THE KINGDOM OF GOD

The Kingdom of God

The Sermon on the Mount

ARCHBISHOP DMITRI

FOREWORD BY PAUL LAZOR

ST VLADIMIR'S SEMINARY PRESS
CRESTWOOD • NEW YORK

*The benefactors would like to dedicate this book with
love to our mothers Edwyn and Sabine.*

LIBRARY OF CONGRESS CATALOGING-IN-PUBLICATION DATA

Royster, Dmitri 1923–
    The kingdom of God : the Sermon on the Mount / by Dmitri Royster.
        p. cm.
    ISBN 0-88141-116-7
    1. Sermon on the Mount—Criticism, interpretation, etc.
    I. Title.
BT380.2.R68   1992   92-29952
226.9'.07—dc20   CIP

ST VLADIMIR'S SEMINARY PRESS
575 Scarsdale Road • Crestwood • New York • 10707
1-800-204-2665
www.svspress.com

ISBN 978-0-88141-116-4

PRINTED IN THE UNITED STATES OF AMERICA

Contents

Foreword

The longest continuous body of the Lord's teachings recorded in the New Testament is known popularly as the Sermon on the Mount. Several years ago Bishop Dmitri published a commentary on this famous Sermon as a series of essays in his diocesan newspaper, *The Dawn*. He now offers us these essays in unified and edited form under the title: *The Kingdom of God*. In them he calls the Sermon on the Mount "more than the 'Magna Carta of the Kingdom,' " and "more than the 'Manifesto of the King,' " but rather "the direct encounter of the human race with revealed truth." This latter perception stands implicitly as a point of reference for many other of the conclusions drawn by the author.

The commentary is certainly a welcome piece of work. It fills a lamentable void in Orthodox scriptural hermeneutics in a fundamental segment of the Bible. It is well written, engaging in style and sufficiently detailed—often singling out specific words or sections of the text in ways which reveal the surprisingly significant in the apparently incidental. This is the kind of treatment accorded, for example, those verses which at first glance appear to be nothing more than a preface to the actual Sermon (Mt 5:1-2). In the commentary, however, the separate phrases and terms of these verses—"and when He was set," "His disciples came unto Him," "He opened His mouth," and "He taught them"—begin to read like liturgical rubrics. They set the appropriate stage; they provide illumination whereby the reader may perceive that it is the Lord Himself who is fulfilling His ministry as *the Teacher*. They echo the words of the psalmist, "It is time for Thee, Lord, to work" (Ps 119: 126 KJV). Interestingly, these same words are addressed by the deacon to the priest as the latter is about to intone the beginning of the Orthodox eucharistic liturgy. Such commentary does more than whet the reader's appetite for further study of the Scripture. It awakens in him a sense of reverence before each of the Bible's words, any one of which may bear an enormity of meaning and direction for one's life.

Similar appreciation is inspired by the author's thorough and scholarly knowledge of the Bible. Frequently focusing on controversial words and phrases, or on those which carry special significance for Christians, Bishop Dmitri explores their meaning in the original Greek or Hebrew. Such attention, for example, is given to the Greek word, *haplous* (cf. Mt 6:22). Convincingly arguing that the word is best translated as *single* ("If...thine eye be *single*, thy whole body shall be full of light"), the Bishop then explains that in this rendition it connects directly with the entire Orthodox tradition of ascetical, moral and spiritual life. Other possible translations, such as "integral," "sincere," "sound," or "healthy," not only come across as shallow, but tend to weaken this connection and to carry the baggage of modern, secularized psychology and emotional reductionism. The Bishop also develops his insights by making extensive cross-references to relevant passages of both the Old and New Testaments. Since most Biblical passages are not cited in their entirety, however, the reader is advised to keep a copy of his personal Bible handy for quick referral and comparison. (Almost without exception, Bishop Dmitri quotes the KJV Bible.)

In the best sense of this word, the entire commentary may be termed *traditional*. Bishop Dmitri consistently discloses that drift or *scope* of Scripture adhered to by the Church throughout the centuries.[1] His expositions are supported by numerous citations of the Church Fathers, particularly Sts John Chrysostom, Ambrose, Augustine and Leo. These citations, however, are not used as mere proof texts to verify the "Orthodoxy" of one or another point of view. They are vivid apprehensions of the Lord's words which remain vital and relevant to the present day. They are expressions of a *living* tradition. They are invitations to an "encounter with revealed truth," the very purpose of the Sermon on the Mount, extended by those whose lives have been engulfed and guided by such an encounter. They summon the reader to transcend the study of the Bible as an accumulation of factual knowledge about the historical Jesus or the observance of religious requirements (as important as such knowledge might be). In the words of Bishop Dmitri, the real fruit of the "encounter with revealed truth" which they engender is "*conversion*": "deliberately choosing to live in accordance with His [God's] will." And conversion is a matter of *love*: a humble and loving repentance before an infi-

---

1 This notion of the "scope of the Divine Scripture" was used by St Athanasius against the Arians and is discussed by Fr. Georges Florovsky in his article, "The Function of Tradition in the Ancient Church," in *Bible, Church, Tradition: An Eastern Orthodox View* (Belmont, MA: Nordland Publishing Co., 1972), pp. 80-83.

nitely humble and loving God. "For God so loved the world that He gave His only-begotten Son, that whoever believes in Him should not perish, but have everlasting life" (Jn 3:16). Conversion also involves a sharing in the life of that particular and, in this world, "separate society" known as *the Church*.

The Church plays a dominant role in determining both the distinctive formulations and the general tone of this commentary. First and most obviously, the author is a *bishop* of the Church. He consistently writes from the perspective of his office in the Church. His aim, shaped by the Church, is essentially *pastoral*: the saving of souls. He urges his flock to follow the "narrow (hard) way" and the "narrow (straight) gate," emphasizing that these are the teachings of Christ most applicable in our day.

Secondly, throughout the commentary Bishop Dmitri demonstrates a consciousness of the difficulties awaiting the people of the Church: those who would follow the narrow and hard way of Christ. This knowledge of his is first hand: the result of the experiences of his own life. While still a teenager Bishop Dmitri came to the Orthodox Church out of a fundamentalist Protestant background. Prior to his episcopal consecration he had a successful career as a university professor. These experiences have made him acutely aware of the allure and entrapments of the fallen world within which, and out of which, a "little flock" has been entrusted to his care. The primary goal of his commentary, therefore, is always churchly and pastoral: the facilitation of a "direct encounter of the human race with revealed truth." This motive also imparts to the commentary a refreshingly contemporary quality: a sense of forcefulness and urgency, of directness and simplicity.

The commentary is theologically engaging as well as spiritually and morally challenging. It does not suffer from ambiguities. Bishops Dmitri is not one to mince words. He says that the Beatitudes are not a "random listing of virtuous attitudes," but rather "God's absolute and eternal moral demands." In another place he refers to them as "first principles": a "logical sequence in which the way of developing the spiritual life is given by our Lord Jesus Christ." Such statements once more exemplify the efforts of an Orthodox bishop to provide simple, sound teaching to a flock engulfed by the moral ambiguities and deviant doctrines of a secularized society with its false prophets (sometimes adorned in the robes of religious leaders) and empty hopes.

> For a bishop must be blameless as a steward of God...holding fast the faithful word as he has been taught, that he may be able, by sound doctrine, both to exhort and to convince those who contradict (Titus 1:7-9).

Bishop Dmitri's fundamentally pastoral concern is further displayed in the organization of the commentary. It follows the logic of the Sermon itself. It is ordered so as to lead a person from reading and *hearing* the Sermon as the words of the Lord, to embracing it fully and striving to accomplish it entirely. In His preaching Jesus Christ calls people to repentance and proclaims the Kingdom of God. This proclamation has elements of both continuity and radical discontinuity with the Law of the Old Testament which preceded it. People are beckoned beyond the impossibilities of the Law to a new Life made accessible in the Son of God now incarnate of the Virgin Mary and the Holy Spirit. This new Life is one of *holiness* and is embarked upon here and now, in this age, in and through the Church.

To those who set out upon the path of holiness and take up their cross, Bishop Dmitri offers ample advice. He devotes particular attention to such areas of contemporary life as job and workplace, money and material possessions, moral issues, ecumenism and the increasing recourse to lawsuits. He also places significant emphasis on the traditional practices of fasting, almsgiving and prayer (each passage of the Lord's Prayer is commented upon). While the Christian life is established on the "foundation of the truth that Christ teaches," the Bishop explains, this life must also be "built." In his view the greatest obstacle to this process of building is *anxiety*: over property as well as assurance about the future. He advises the reader to live in the present: "In a total commitment to God, with faith and joy, the future is always bright."

With a simplicity and directness which typify the tone of the entire commentary, Bishop Dmitri responds to the age-old question about what a person must do to inherit the eternal life of the Kingdom of God (Mt 19:16). He says:

> Nothing could be clearer—he must do the will of his Father in heaven. The profession of faith, the claim to be a follower of Jesus Christ must be followed up by the kind of life...of which Jesus speaks through the Sermon on the Mount.

Fr. Paul Lazor
St Vladimir's Seminary

I

Proclamation of the Kingdom

Chapter 1

The holy apostle Matthew tells us that our Lord Jesus Christ began His public ministry with the proclamation of the kingdom of God: "Repent, for the kingdom of heaven (of God) is at hand."

This preaching of Christ did not begin until after His baptism—at which He was revealed to be the Son of God, one of the Holy Trinity—and after His temptation by the devil, in which he was seen to be perfectly obedient to the will of God.

When St Matthew prefaces the first public utterance of Jesus with the expression, "From that time, Jesus began to preach and to say..." he specifically refers to the time when the Lord heard that John the Baptist had been imprisoned.

John had declared that "He that cometh after me is greater than me" (Mt 3:11). This is the forerunner's last prophetic declaration. His ministry gave way to that of the One who was the object not only of his prophecy but also those of all the prophets before him. In the Gospel according to St John, the Baptist declares that his ministry is completed: "He must increase, but I must decrease" (3:30). St Luke emphasizes the difference between the preaching of John and that of Jesus: "The law and the prophets were until John: since that time the kingdom of God is preached, and every man presseth into it" (16:16).

The first declaration of Christ, "Repent, for the kingdom of heaven is at hand," has several important meanings. The first Gospel records this as both the essence and the theme of the Baptist's preaching (3:2). Thus, Jesus authenticates the preaching of His forerunner; He identifies Himself as the One about whom John had been preaching.

It also makes clear the purpose of His becoming flesh and dwelling among us: the kingdom of heaven has drawn near. Reconciliation, communion with God, and salvation are accessible to all mankind. Heaven has come to earth, because the Son of God Himself has become man, lives among men and deals directly with them.

Although the presence of the kingdom may not always have been discerned at first, even by the apostles, the Lord gives three of them a direct revelation of Himself, His glory and power, in the Transfiguration. His words just before the dazzling event on Mt. Tabor leave no doubt as to the relationship between His presence and the coming of the kingdom: "There be some of them that stand here, which shall not taste of death, till they have seen the kingdom of God come with power" (Mk 9:1), or "till they see the Son of Man coming in His kingdom" (Mt 16:28), or "till they see the kingdom of God" (Lk 9:27).

The essential condition for access to the kingdom is given at the same time—Repent. Man cannot be reconciled with God, have communion with Him, or expect salvation without a profound change of mind (or heart). In other words, he must adopt a whole new view of things, a whole new attitude, recognizing his sinful condition, being sorry for it, acknowledging his need for the Savior and putting his trust in Him.

After calling His disciples, Jesus continued His preaching, primarily in the synagogues, for it was to the Jews that He came first. It was they whom He had prepared for His coming for centuries. The heart of His message was always "the gospel of the kingdom" (Mt 4:23; Lk 8:1). He also sent His disciples out to heal and to preach just as He was doing (Lk 9:2; Mt 10:7). What did He tell them emphatically to declare? That the kingdom of God is "come nigh unto you" (Lk 10:9).

And so it continued throughout His earthly ministry (Mt 4:23; 9:35; Mk 1:14). All of his references to the kingdom are far too numerous to list here, but in them we may distinguish three meanings for the "kingdom." In one sense, it is life in God, a following of God's commandments and His righteousness (Mt 6:33; Lk 12:31). This is the idea of so many of the parables, in which He says that the kingdom of heaven is like (among other things) a grain of mustard seed, leaven, treasure hid in a field, and a merchant seeking fine pearls (Mt 13). In the Beatitudes, we see that the kingdom is attained by poverty of spirit and by suffering persecution for righteousness' sake (Mt 5:3, 10). And perhaps most important of all is His declaration that the kingdom of God is within you (Lk 17:21).

The kingdom also comes to man directly through God's intervention in the world. We begin to understand that God is establishing a society in the world separate from the world. It was to His disciples that He said, "Fear not, little flock: for it is your Father's pleasure to give you the kingdom" (Lk 12:32). Jesus had set up His kingdom among men by revealing to them what the real life of man was to be according to the will of God. It is clear also that He regarded those who were His followers as constituting a kingdom distinct from the world around it. St John records Jesus' answer to Pilate with regard to His kingship: "My kingdom is not of this world; if my kingdom were of his world, then would my servants fight, that I should not be delivered to the Jews: but now my kingdom is not from hence." In the great priestly prayer which the same Evangelist records (Jn 17:6, 16) the Lord declares that "the men which thou gavest me out of the world...are not of the world." (Obviously, they were still in it.)

CHAPTER 2

We have explored two of the three different but interrelated meanings of the Kingdom of heaven that we are able to discern in our Lord's teaching. The first is the kingdom of God as already present in those who believe in Christ and live according to His will in His Church, in the power of the Holy Spirit. The second is the kingdom as a separate society (the Church) in the world, whose home and destiny is Christ's eternal kingdom in the age to come. Before going on to the third meaning of the kingdom, we feel it important to devote a part of our discussion to the Lord's kingship itself.

Jesus was born as King of the Jews. The magi came seeking to worship Him as such. "Where is He that is born King of the Jews?" (Mt 2:2). The angel announced to the all-holy Virgin: "The Lord God shall give unto Him the throne of His father David: and He shall reign over the house of Jacob for ever; and of His kingdom there shall be no end" (Lk 1:32-33). Although He rejected attempts to make Him a "king" in any worldly sense (Jn 6:15), He accepted the acclaim of the people of Jerusalem as he entered that city just before His Passion: "Blessed be the King that cometh in the name of the Lord" (Lk 19:38; see also Mt 21:9, Mk 11:9-10, and Jn 12:13-15). Then in answer to Pilate's question at the trial, Jesus accepted the title itself: "Thou sayest that I am king. To this end was I born..." (Jn 18:37) and Pilate ordered, over the protests of the Jews, that the inscription on the Cross be "Jesus of Nazareth, King of the Jews."

But this was not kingship as some of the Jews had expected it. The kingdom of God was within but not of this world, and the leaders of this world could not comprehend it. Those who enjoyed the reputation of being "religious," the leaders of Israel, were not pleasing to God. Indeed, those they scorned are more acceptable to God than they: "Verily I say unto you, that the publicans and the harlots go into the kingdom of God before you" (Mt 21:31)" They heard His terrible judgment, when He gave the parable of the vineyard: "Therefore say I unto you, The kingdom of God shall be taken from you, and given to a nation bringing forth the fruits thereof" (Mt 21:43). They knew that he was speaking of them (v.45).

The Kingdom of Christ, while it is present now in men and women who lead a godly life, and while it is also identical with the "separate society" within but called out of this world—the Church—it is the eternal reign of Christ (Lk 1:33) that will be initiated with His second coming (Mt 25:31-46).

Numerous passages in the Gospels indicate that the Kingdom of Christ is not only already begun in this age, but also belongs to the age to come. Others spoke to Him of the kingdom as a future reality, and far from rejecting the idea, He shows by His answers that they were not mistaken. For example, the mother of Zebedee's children asked for special places for her two sons in His kingdom. Although He predicted that they would undergo the same suffering as He, He also said: "But to sit on my right hand, and on my left, is not mine to give, but it shall be given to them for whom it is prepared of my Father" (Mt 20:21-23). In another case, the wise thief crucified with the Lord asked Him, "Lord, remember me when thou comest into thy kingdom. And Jesus said unto him, Verily I say unto thee. Today shalt thou be with me in paradise" (Lk 23:42-43).

Jesus also teaches that all those who forsake everything and follow Him will receive spiritual rewards for their devotion in the present life and in the world to come. "There is no man that hath left house, or parents, or brethren, or wife, or children, for the kingdom of God's sake, who shall not receive manifold more in this present time, and in the world to come life everlasting" (Lk 8:29-30).

The Kingdom that Christ establishes is realized in the present but will be realized in its fullness in the world to come. "And I appoint unto you a kingdom, as my Father hath appointed unto me; that ye may eat and drink at my table in my kingdom" (Lk 22:29-30). Those who belong to Christ's kingdom on earth, the Church, eat and drink at His table in the Eucharist, which is itself an anticipation of the Messianic banquet of the age to come. His promise to the apostles that they will also sit on those thrones judging the twelve tribes of Israel obviously corresponds to a future reality.

In the forty days following the Resurrection, according to St Luke's testimony (Acts 1:3), Jesus spoke to the disciples of the things pertaining to the kingdom of God. What He said to them no doubt had to do with the kingdom that they enjoyed, His presence, and with the Church that would be His continued presence in the world after the Ascension, as well as with the kingdom fully realized after the end of time.

Later, St Paul would explain the relationship between the "Kingdom of Christ" and the "Kingdom of God." "Then cometh the end, when He shall have delivered up the kingdom to God, when He shall have put down all rule and all authority and power" (1 Cor 5:24). Thus the completion of the work of Christ, the God-Man, is seen as the gathering together in His Kingdom of men and women, His fellows, from out of this world, and of His presenting it to the Father as the final act of His work both as Priest and King. Then will the kingdom established by Christ be identical with the kingdom of God.

CHAPTER 3

St Matthew's introduction to that great body of Jesus' teaching, which we commonly call "the Sermon on the Mount," is a short and seemingly very simple statement: "And seeing the multitude, He went up into a mountain; and when He was set, His disciples came unto Him, and He opened His mouth, and taught them..." (5:1-2).

In spite of this statement's brevity, most of the Fathers of the Church who have left us commentaries on the "Sermon" have found it to be filled with significance. For them (St John Chrysostom and St Augustine, for example), every phrase of these two verses is said with a purpose, in order to provide the proper framework for the account of the Lord's teaching.

"Seeing the multitude"—Jesus, as a result of His preaching and healing, often found Himself followed by great crowds of people. This incident is one of several in which, although His compassion is never lacking and He even heals the multitudes, He seems to be eager to withdraw and even hide from them (see Mk 3:9, Lk 5:16 and Jn 12:36). In view of Jesus' whole teaching ministry, we can only come to the conclusion that He had His own "timetable" for His work and for the revelation of His identity. We should also remember that on a number of occasions, He warned the disciples or others not to tell anyone what He had done or what they had witnessed (Mt 8:4, 16:20; 7:9; Mk 7:36; 8:26,30: 9:9; Lk 5:14; 8:56; 9;21). Jesus withdrew from the multitude in this case for a specific purpose, as we shall see below.

"He went up into a mountain"—The Fathers see more in the mountain than a simple place to hide. Since Jesus is about to reveal all the fundamental points of His teaching, to give His new law, He goes up to a mountain, just as Moses had gone up to the mountain when he gave the old law. There is, however, an essential difference between them: Moses went up to the mountain to receive the law from God, so that he might convey it to the people. Jesus, who is the Lawgiver Himself, from whom the old law had come, goes up to the mountain now to give His new law.

St John tells us that the law was given by Moses, but grace and truth came by Jesus Christ (1:17). Jesus Himself declares that He is the true Bread of life that came down from heaven. Moses, on the other hand, was but an instrument of God's care for His people, and the bread they received from heaven through him was symbolic of the true Bread from heaven. (See Jn 6:32-35.)

"And when He was set"—St Augustine says that "He teaches sitting down for this is proper to the dignity of the teaching office." It might be appropriate likewise to point out that Jesus sat because He was not only the man whom they all saw, but He was also the eternal God. He is not communicating some other's teaching, but His very own. Any place where He sat would be in a very real sense the throne of God.

"His disciples came unto Him"—The purpose of Jesus' withdrawal from the crowd was without doubt that He might declare His will first exclusively to those whom He had chosen to be His apostles, the ones whom He would send to proclaim His will. He thus shows that they, who will form His Church, will be initiated into the mysteries of the kingdom (Lk 8:10) and that He will send His Church to proclaim the nearness of the kingdom (Mt 10:7) and to continue His work (Jn 20:21).

"He opened His mouth"—As obvious as it is that in order to teach one must "open his mouth," the Evangelist seems to think it is important to say so as he sets out to write down the Lord's teachings. For St John Chrysostom, its inclusion is not without purpose. He says that even in the Lord's silence He never stopped giving instruction. His very presence and the way in which He moved about among men and dealt with them were all eloquent "sermons."

Finally, the Gospel says "He taught them." It was the disciples whom He taught first, but His message is intended for all mankind. Just as God has chosen to reveal the truth about Himself and about humanity by becoming man Himself, He chooses to continue to use the human voice, that of His apostles, to extend His truth all over the world.

What follows is, in St Augustine's words, "the perfect pattern of the Christian life," the fundamental standard of behavior for all those who follow Christ. The principles contained in the "sermon" are God's moral demands on mankind. The truths revealed in it are absolute and eternal; they cannot be altered or adjusted to fit the times, even though there are those who call themselves Christians today who try to do just that.

CHAPTER 4

The Lord began His public preaching by declaring the nearness of the kingdom of heaven. The "kingdom," as He used the term, refers to man's spiritual state when he experiences the presence of God, to the society (the Church) which He specifically called out of this world's society, and to the life with God in the world to come. We must, however, understand that there are attitudes or states of mind that are necessary for attaining the kingdom, and are manifest in those who become partakers of it.

Jesus, as the final and greatest prophet, proclaimed more perfectly than all the prophets who preceded Him the truth about mankind. Jesus' teachings are full of surprises for the secular point of view. Those things which He declares and shows to be virtues were and still are rejected: the people He calls blessed (or "happy") the world would call wretched. Perhaps this is why the Greek word *makarios* is best translated "blessed"; "happy" could be understood in a material sense.

Such was the case with the world into which Jesus was born—the Jewish religious world and the Roman political world. Apparently, many Jews had come to understand the messianic expectation of their own tradition in secular terms. Formal membership in the nation-church of Israel, as well as formal compliance with ritual and moral requirements, was sufficient. Their well-being was usually considered proof of their piety and of God's favor. For the Roman, the state was in itself a god for the people: every individual had as his first duty service to the state and was individually expendable. Strength, bravery, ambition, pride and self-centeredness were laudable, accepted virtues for the citizen of the Empire.

The Lord often shocked His hearers and the witnesses of His acts, even His disciples, when He revealed God's standards concerning life and interpersonal relationships. On a number of occasions His followers even objected when He offended their human sense of equity and justice.

When Jesus took His disciples apart from the multitude to reveal to them the essence of His teaching, in His first extended sermon, He began by declaring certain attitudes, states and aspirations as signs of the godly person's life and as means for attaining the kingdom which He had proclaimed. He described as "blessed" those who possessed these attitudes and states of mind. The blessedness of which He speaks is the happiness that belongs to those who experience the reign of God in their lives; it is a happiness by which they come to know the happiness of the world to come, where God's presence will be enjoyed in the fullest sense.

From a purely human point of view, it would be difficult to understand how people described by these Beatitudes could be happy, except perhaps insofar as they might get a kind of self-satisfaction out of their "piety." This is certainly not the point of the Beatitudes, for such was the feeling of the Pharisee in the parable (Lk 18:10), whose pride was specifically condemned by the Lord.

The "poor in spirit" are the humble, those who are conscious of their own sins and of their dependence on God, not on their own resources, for spiritual growth and for meaning in their lives. They realize that they must ask God for forgiveness of their sins. Humility before God also implies humility before one's fellows, and the starting point for humility is love, love of God and love of one's neighbor. The question, "How can one love God, whom he hath not seen, when he loveth not his brother, whom he hath seen?" (1 Jn 4:20) might also be stated in these terms: "How can one be humble before God, whom he hath not seen, when he is not humble before his brother whom he hath seen?"

"They that mourn" are not just sentimental people who weep at the slightest provocation, but those who weep (or are deeply sorry) for their sins. They also weep for the sins of others, but here too, it is not a question of self-righteousness or judgment, but of love and compassion.

The "meek" are those who live, conscious of their own unworthiness, with patience and in peace with their fellow men. Those who live in hostility with others cannot enter the kingdom of God, the new earth which the meek shall inherit.

"They which do hunger and thirst after righteousness" are those who "seek first the kingdom of God and His righteousness" (Mt 6:33). They long for God's justice and truth, not only for themselves, but for all others as well. These people may not be filled at all in the earthly sense, but are assuredly in a spiritual way.

"The merciful" are those who, because of their love, know how to forgive. It is they who obtain mercy, the ultimate mercy, salvation of their souls and the kingdom of God. The Lord said, "If ye forgive men their trespasses, your heavenly Father will forgive you your trespasses." (Mt 6:14)

CHAPTER 5

The Fathers of the Church, notably St Ambrose, find in the Beatitudes not a random listing of virtuous attitudes or states of mind, but an orderly, logical sequence in which the way of developing the spiritual life is given by our Lord Jesus Christ. Each of the virtues is necessary for and produces the one that follows. Poverty of spirit is not only the first in the list, but is the first in importance, the one without which none of the others may be acquired. It has to do with the conquest of the most basic of man's sins, his pride. Poverty of spirit begets meekness. (Both St Ambrose and St Augustine give this as the second, although in Matthew, it is third.) Meekness is humility (the opposite of pride), gentleness and modesty. Meekness makes one conscious of his unworthiness and his sins, and for these he weeps—not necessarily outwardly, but certainly inwardly, in the spirit. When one weeps for or mourns his sinfulness, he has a hunger and a thirst for righteousness (or "justice"), for all that is right and just, in accordance with God's will, not his own will. The fruit of righteousness is mercy, which includes compassion for the other in all his failings and his weaknesses, and willingness to forgive. Righteousness and mercy are perfectly joined together, and one is able to be merciful only if he has a pure heart. Showing mercy contributes to the cleansing of the heart.

Concerning the "pure in heart" (*katharoi*, literally "clean," in Greek), St Augustine says: "Let a man do all

that has been said till now (in the first five Beatitudes),
and his heart will be clean." St Leo the Great expresses
the same idea: "And what does it mean to have a clean
heart, if not to practice those virtues of which we have
just spoken?"

The "heart" is considered—not only here, but generally—the seat of a person's inmost being. "It is with the
heart that a person appreciates what is essential, that he
chooses and determines his life" (Semionoff, *Adult Cate-
chism*). Its cleansing or purification signifies the transformation that makes it possible to "see God."

It is by faith that hearts are purified, as the Apostle
Peter declares in the dispute over the circumcision of
Gentile converts (Acts 15:9). Not only must one make
every effort to purify his heart, but he must seek God's
help in order to acquire this essential characteristic of the
new life in Christ. David the Psalmist says: "Create in me
a clean heart, O God: and renew a right spirit within me"
(Ps 50(51):11). St Augustine advises us: "It may be that
you find it hard to purify your heart. Call upon Him, and
He will not disdain to make there a clean abode for
himself, and come to dwell with you" (*On the Eight
Sentences of the Beatitudes from the Gospel*).

Finally, cleanness of heart means simply holiness,
and we cannot forget that the aim of the life in Christ is
to be holy, or "perfect," as the Lord Himself commands
us (Mt 5:48). In the Epistle to the Hebrews, the Apostle
is really saying that purity of heart and holiness are the
same, in view of his admonition that without holiness one
cannot "see God" (Heb 12:14). Blessed are the pure in
heart; for they shall see God.

One of the first fruits of holiness is the desire for peace and the effort to make peace. "Who are the peace-makers?" asks St Augustine.

They who make peace. Do you see others quarrel-ling? Be the servant of peace between them. Say to one man what is good about another; and to the other speak well of the first. Do you hear evil spoken of one by another who is angry? Do not betray what you hear. Close your ears to the outcry of an angry man; offer him the enduring counsel of peace (*Op. Cit.*).

In order to accomplish this, however, it is necessary to have peace within oneself, and the way to achieve this is to accept without question the will of God.

St Leo the Great gives us more insight into the words of the Lord concerning peacemakers.

This blessedness is not promised to every kind of agreement, nor every sort of concord; but to that of which the apostle says: Let us have peace with God (Rom 5:1: 2 Cor 13:11); and that of which the Prophet David says: Much peace have they that love thy law; and to them there is no stumbling-block (Ps 118:165). The closest bond of friendship, the closest affinity of mind and heart, cannot truly claim this peace; if these ties are not in conformity with the will of God. Excluded from the dignity of this peace are they who are linked one with the other by shameless desires, those joined together for the purposes of crime and evil doing. There is no concord between the love of this world and the love of God; and he shall not belong to the children of God who will not separate himself from the children of this world. But they who at all times have God in mind (Tobias 4:6), careful to keep the unity of the spirit in the bond of peace (Eph 4:3), are never in conflict with the eternal law, saying in the prayer of faith, Thy will be done on earth as it is in heaven. These are the peacemakers, these indeed are of one mind, and dwell in holy harmony, and shall be called by the eternal name of 'sons of God,' and joint heirs with Christ (Rom 8:17): for this shall be the reward of the love of God and the love of our neighbor, that we shall suffer no more adversity, and go no more in fear of scandals, but with all struggle of temptation at an end, we shall rest in the most serene peace of God (*Homily on the Steps of the Ascent to Blessedness*).

CHAPTER 6

As the great and last Prophet, our Lord Jesus Christ proclaimed God's will for the human race. As the perfect Man, He put that will into practice, so that man might not only hear of his ideal and authentic way of life, but also witness it.

The Beatitudes are the very foundation of this way of life; they contain the fundamental spiritual qualities and behavior patterns which should distinguish or characterize the follower of Christ. (Thus it is easy to understand why the Church has given them such a prominent place, as the third antiphon, in the Divine Liturgy.) Not only does the Lord declare those who possess these qualities and practice these things to be blessed, but He also promises them a certain reward.

Until now we have said little about the reward (note the singular), but have rather devoted our attention to those things whose possessors are called blessed by our Lord. It does seem important, however, to consider briefly the nature of His promises before going on to talk about the last two Beatitudes.

The reward is not a material one, but a spiritual one, and it has a direct relationship to the Lord's original proclamation, the first thing He announced as He opened His work: The kingdom of heaven is at hand. Even before the Sermon on the Mount, in which the Beatitudes are declared, Jesus went about all Galilee, teaching in their synagogues, and preaching the gospel of the kingdom (Mt 4:23). The "poor in spirit" are told that the kingdom of heaven is theirs, belongs to them; the "pure in heart" shall see God, i.e., shall be with Him in His kingdom; the "peacemakers" will be called the children of God, "children of the kingdom." The "earth" that the meek shall inherit is not the old earth as we know it, but the new earth, when Christ comes in His kingdom. Comfort, being filled, and obtaining mercy are the reward of the kingdom, for they will be granted to those who receive the blessed, eternal life from Christ.

St John Chrysostom speaks of the reward in these terms:

> But even though you do not hear of a kingdom given in each one of the blessings, do not be discouraged. For although He gave different names to the rewards, yet He brings all into His kingdom. Thus, both when He says, "they that mourn shall be comforted;" and, "they that show mercy shall obtain mercy;" and, "the pure in heart shall see God;" and, the peacemakers "shall be called the children of God;" nothing else but the Kingdom does he represent by all these sayings... (*On Matthew*, Homily xv).

In the eighth Beatitude, "Blessed are they which are persecuted for righteousness' sake...," we find the Lord's first mention of the persecution which His followers will be called to suffer. Their seeking God's kingdom and His righteousness (Mt 6:33), their putting this pursuit first, above all other concerns, will be the cause of their persecution. And the reward promised is, "for theirs in the kingdom of heaven," exactly as He had stated it in the first Beatitude.

The ninth Beatitude is not stated any longer in general terms, but is addressed personally to the disciples themselves: "Blessed are ye..." They will have the special privilege of being persecuted for His sake, because they will be the teachers of His way. The Lord, therefore, is without any doubt, promising them that the earthly reward for their obedience to God's will, for their seeing the world and their relations with others with His eyes, will be reproach, hatred and oppression. We must take note, however, that the blessedness is gained by Christ's disciples because of being falsely maligned and *precisely for their following of Him.*

> Lest you think that the mere fact of being spoken evil of makes men blessed, He has set two limitations; when it is for His sake, and when the things that are said are false; for without these, he who is evil spoken of, so far from being blessed, is miserable (St John Chrysostom, *On Matthew*, Homily xv).

Thus, at the beginning of the Lord's prophetic ministry, He does not hesitate to prepare His disciples for the persecution that will surely be their lot. St Luke records this saying of Jesus in a more forceful manner: "Blessed are ye, when men shall hate you, and when they shall separate you (from their company), and shall reproach you, and cast out your name as evil, for the Son of Man's sake" (Lk 6:22). The Lord Himself was persecuted for His declaration of the will of God for mankind, since "man has his own righteousness" (Rom 10:3), and even more for His own obedience to that will. "If the world hate you, ye know that it hated me before...Remember the word that I said unto you, the servant is not greater than his Lord. If they have persecuted me, they will also persecute you; if they have kept my saying, they will keep yours also, But all these things will they do unto you for my sake, because they know not Him that sent me" (Jn 15:18, 20-21).

In fact, the Apostles did experience the rejection and ill-treatment that the Lord foretold. They might have found favor with the world—"The world would love his own" (Jn 15:19)—if, out of fear or a desire to please society, they had ceased preaching in His name. But they proved to be worthy of their calling: "...And when they had called the apostles and beaten them, they commanded that they should not speak in the name of Jesus, and let them go. And they departed from the presence of the council, rejoicing that they were counted worthy to suffer shame for His name. And daily in the temple, and in every house, they ceased not to teach and preach Jesus Christ" (Acts 5:40-42).

St Paul encourages the Christians at Corinth, reminding them that the persecutions they were undergoing were for a time only, but that their faithfulness will be rewarded with everlasting life (2 Cor 4:17).

The Lord does not proceed with His teaching without first offering the disciples the greatest consolation: "Rejoice and be exceeding glad, for great is your reward in heaven." Then, He adds a fact from history in which they should take both comfort and encouragement, establishing a link between them and the great prophets of the Old Covenant: "For so persecuted they the prophets which were before you."

CHAPTER 7

After having shown the disciples the inevitable consequences (reproach, rejection and persecution) of following Him and His way, the Lord emphasizes the responsibility they will have for the work He will send them to do in His name.

"Ye are the salt of the earth: but if the salt have lost his savor, wherewith shall it be salted? It is thenceforth good for nothing, but to be cast out, and to be trodden under foot of men. Ye are the light of the world. A city that is set on a hill cannot be hid. Neither do men light a candle, and put it under a bushel, but on a candlestick; and it giveth light to all that are in the house. Let your light so shine before men, that they may see your good works, and glorify your Father which is in heaven" (Mt 5:13-16).

Jesus came into a world that was fallen and corrupt through sin. The very purpose of His coming was to restore what mankind had lost by willful disobedience. His work was to set the human race free from evil and the decay that resulted from it, to win the victory over death, which is "the wages of sin," as St Paul says (Rom 6:23), and to lead all people to their original destiny, communion with God. Not only was this divine plan to be accomplished by God's actual intervention into man's world, but it also included the participation of the human race. It now begins to be clear that He had chosen certain men to continue the work that He would accomplish. He will say to them at the conclusion of the period of His earthly ministry, "As the Father hath sent me, even so send I you" (Jn 20:21).

The lost, fallen world then will depend quite literally on the ministry of these especially chosen disciples. They will even be accountable for the world's salvation. The earth, as it were, had "lost its savor"; all human nature had lost it. Salt is the substance that gives flavor or enlivens what otherwise is insipid and even dead. It is a way of saying that the earth without God is a meaningless place and the men and women that inhabit it lead a pointless existence. So, because of the disciples' faith and their godly life—the essence of which He had given in the Beatitudes, the very first principles that He taught—they will be charged with conveying His truth to the rest of mankind.

Here, at the beginning of the Lord's teaching ministry, He reveals the purpose of the Church, for those men that He had called out of the ordinary, common pursuits of life constituted the Church from the beginning. Nowhere is the meaning of the word "ecclesia" clearer than it is when He went about choosing His disciples with the simple command, "Follow me." (Such is the meaning of the Greek word—the group of "those who have been called out.") It was in this way that Jesus began to prepare the Church for its essential work in the world.

Not only does He use the figure "salt" to reveal the disciples' relation to the rest of the world, but He goes on to call them "the light of the world." Just as He was the true light which shone in the darkness of the world that had lost its light (Jn 1:4-9), He now begins to tell them, perhaps to their amazement, that they too were to be that light.

The disciples, however, are not called "the salt of the earth" and "the light of the world" without first being warned of the possibility of not living up to their vocation. They, as teachers, are to give "savor" and "light" to the world, but obviously they, also being mortals and subject to temptation, could fail. If they, the salt, lose their savor, there is nothing with which to salt them. If they, the light, hide their light and fail to lighten the world, then the world still remains in darkness. St Augustine expands Jesus' admonition "but if the salt have lost his savor, wherewith shall it be salted?" He writes,

> If you, through whom the nations to some degree are to be kept from corruption; if you, out of fear of earthly persecutions, should lose the kingdom of heaven; there will be no one who can remove your error, since God has chosen you to remove the error of others (*Our Lord's Sermon on the Mount*, Chapter 6).

St John Chrysostom records Jesus' warning about the light in this way:

> I, it is true, have kindled the light, but its continuing to burn, let that come of your diligence: not for your own sakes alone, but also for the sake of those who are to profit by these rays, and to be guided to the truth. Since calumnies surely shall not be able to obscure your brightness, if you be still living a strict life, as becomes those who are to convert the whole world; show forth, therefore, a life worthy of His

grace; that even as it is preached everywhere, so this light may everywhere accompany the same (Homily 15, *On the Gospel of Matthew*).

Further, the purpose of their mission is contained in the concluding exhortation of this second section of the Sermon: "Let your light so shine before men, that they may see your good works, and glorify your Father which is in heaven." He tells the disciples that the purpose of their following the virtuous path He has described to them is not that they may be praised by others. The particular aim of the Christian life is, first of all, to please God by obeying His will, and then to make those who see the Christian's good works glorify God. In other words, the true disciple of Christ will be able to accomplish his task in such a way that men are brought to God.

The passage we have just considered can be regarded as an introduction to the rather extended section that follows (vv. 17-48). Here the disciples are instructed in the way in which they and all Christians may truly become "the salt of the earth" and "the light of the world."

II

The Law and the Gospel

CHAPTER 8

In Matthew 5:17, Jesus makes His first reference of which we have knowledge to the Law: "Think not that I am come to destroy the law and the prophets..." However, we find that St. Luke records another saying of His, which seems to reduce the Law to a kind of preparation for the preaching of the Gospel and to imply that the Gospel would replace the Law: "The law and the prophets were until John: since that time the Kingdom of God is preached..." (16:17). Further, the Gospel of John seems to place the law and the Gospel in opposition: The law "was given by Moses," John writes, "but grace and truth came by Jesus Christ" (Jn 1:17). St Paul, who knew the Law perhaps better than the other apostles and was a zealous defender of it before his conversion, solves the problem of the relation between the Law and the Gospel in these terms: The Law was our schoolmaster to bring us unto Christ, that we might be justified by faith (Gal 3:24). For him, a faithful following of Christ and His doctrine is a confirmation of the Law: "Do we make void the law through faith? God forbid; yea, we establish the law" (Rom 3:31).

This section of the Sermon on the Mount (Mt 5:17-20) contains an essential explanation of the relation between the Kingdom proclaimed by Jesus and the Old Testament. He is about to reveal the new law; the writer of Hebrews will say later that a change in the priesthood had required a change in the law (7:12). The Jews, even if they did not keep the law, held it in such high esteem as the complete and final revelation of God to man that it would be difficult for them to accept as the promised Messiah a man whose announced purpose was to replace the law of Moses by another. It was

41

then perhaps to allay their fears and to anticipate their objection that He declared that He had not come to destroy but to fulfill. (In Greek "plerosai" means "to complete" and "to make perfect.") As we shall see later, He does indeed confirm the moral precepts of the law, but He will also reveal the spirit of those precepts.

It is important also to note that He claims for Himself authority over the commandments. This we understand by His repetition before each of the six examples that follow: "Ye have heard that it was said to them of old time...but I say unto you..." (verses 21-22: 27-28: 31-32; 33-34; 38-39; and 43-44). The Church has always taught that the Word of God was the Lawgiver, the one who spoke to Moses when the commandments were given originally. So, when He came into the world and "dwelt among men," he completed, according to His wisdom and His plan, what He had revealed. Essentially what He taught was that doing God's will was not a simple matter of compliance with laws, but rather of obedience and love, of heartfelt conversion.

Before going on to discuss the other three verses (28-30) of this section of chapter 5, it will be instructive to consider the ways in which Jesus did "fulfil the law and the prophets." The following paragraphs are taken from St John Chrysostom's sixteenth homily on the Gospel of St Matthew:

> The prophets He fulfilled, in that He confirmed by the events of His life and His actions all that had been said concerning Him: for this reason, the Evangelist usually says in each case: that it might be fulfilled which was spoken by the prophet(s)...

But the law He fulfilled, not in one way only, but in a second and third also. In one way, by transgressing none of the precepts of the Law. For [proof] that He did fulfil it all, hear what He says to John the Baptist: For thus it becometh us to fulfil all righteousness [Mt 3:15: "righteousness " here means the ritual purifications such as circumcision and baptism]. And to the Jews also He said: which of you convinceth (reprove or convict) me of sin (Jn 8:46). And to the disciples again: The prince of this world (the devil) cometh and findeth nothing (no sin) in me (so as to claim me) (Jn 14:30). And the prophet too, centuries before, had said of Him: He did no sin (Is 53:9).

In another sense, He fulfilled the Law by granting the possibility of fulfilling it to those who believe in Him. He judged sin in the flesh, that the righteousness of the law might be fulfilled in us who walk not after the flesh (Rom 8:34). For the Law was striving toward this, to make men righteous, but had not the power to do so.

He came and brought in the way of righteousness by faith, and so established what the Law had aspired to...

But if any one will inquire accurately, he will also find another, a third sense, in which this had been done...in the code of laws which He was about to deliver to them. For His sayings were not a repeal of the former, but a drawing out and filling up of them.

CHAPTER 9

Jesus revealed that the purpose of His coming was to fulfill the law and the prophets: this He did by observing the law Himself, revealing its true spirit or meaning, and perfecting it. He fulfilled the prophesies in that He did exactly what they had foretold of Him.

He now emphasizes the enduring nature of the law and the necessity for the whole of it to be fulfilled: "Verily, I say unto you till heaven and earth pass, one jot or one tittle shall in no wise pass from the law, till all be fulfilled" (Mt 5:18). Not even the smallest detail is to go unfulfilled. The "jot" (*iota* in Greek) refers to the Hebrew letter "yodh," literally the smallest of the 22 consonants, and "tittle" (*Keraia* in Greek) probably means a simple decorative writing device. The point of the Lord's saying is obvious: He means the whole law.

The law is confirmed by Jesus, and we are to understand by this that its moral precepts are not in any way relative to any time or place: they are absolute because they are from God. They will endure until the end of time, "till heaven and earth pass," and before that final event, all the prophecies of the Old Testament will come to pass.

He still does not depart from the basic theme of His preaching, the kingdom of heaven, when He warns: "Whosoever therefore shall break one of these least commandments, and shall teach men so, he shall be called the least in the kingdom of heaven; but whosoever shall do and teach them, the same shall be called great in the kingdom of heaven" (v. 19).

Two things are of special interest here: first, the idea of "least" commandments, implying that some are weightier than others. In fact, there was a popular rabbinical distinction between "heavy" and "light" commandments in the law. The holy fathers, however, do not seem to think that the Lord had this in mind when He referred to "these least commandments." The apostle James gives us the key to understanding the Lord's intention when he writes: "For whosoever shall keep the whole law, and yet offend in one (point), he is guilty of all" (Jas 2:10).

The second interesting point in this verse is that one who breaks one of these "least commandments, and shall teach men so, shall be called least in the kingdom of heaven." Could this mean that such a transgressor does have a place, albeit an inferior one, in the kingdom? The Fathers (such as St John Chrysostom and St Augustine) seem to be in agreement concerning the meaning of the Lord's reference to the kingdom in this declaration. They think He simply alludes to the time of the general resurrection and of the awesome coming again (Chrysostom, Hom. xvi, *On Matthew*). St John Chrysostom goes on to point out that it would be inconsistent with the Lord's teaching to assign some place, however "least," in the kingdom to one who deliberately breaks the law and tries to entice others to do the same. At the time of the coming of the kingdom in its fullness and power, he will simply be condemned. In this way, he will be the "least."

It is not the old law, imperfectly practiced by the teachers, scribes and pharisees, but the perfected and completed law that the disciples were to do and to teach. Their righteousness must be greater than that of the old teachers, many of whom no doubt complied with its requirements. Now, however, it is not a question of that kind of observance, but of submission of the will to God, a complete conversion to Him and His way. Without this, it will be impossible to enter the Kingdom of Heaven. For a faithful following of the law, as understood in the Old Testament, the reward was a material one: prosperity, earthly well-being and happiness. After Christ's coming, we understand that this kind of reward was only symbolic or a "type" (for it would only be temporary) of the ultimate reward, eternal life in the kingdom. Such is, after all, the meaning of all the Old Testament "types." St John Chrysostom has this to say: "It is no longer a land that floweth with milk and honey, nor a comfortable old age, nor many children, nor corn and wine, and flocks and herds: but Heaven, and the good things in the Heavens, and adoption and brotherhood with the Only-begotten, and to partake of the inheritance and to be glorified and to reign with Him, and those unnumbered rewards. And as to our having received greater help (the grace of the All Holy Spirit), hear St Paul when he says, There is therefore no condemnation now to them which are in Christ Jesus, who walk not after the flesh, but after the Spirit: for the law of the Spirit of life hath made me free from the law of sin and death" (Rom 8:1,2) (Hom. xvi, *On Matthew*).

CHAPTER 10

As we have seen, our Lord Jesus Christ did not come to destroy the law and the prophets, but to fulfill them. In the course of His teaching ministry, He not only did not abolish any of the commandments; He strengthened them and revealed their spirit and true meaning. It became clear to those who heard Him that the commandments were not given to lay a heavy, impossible burden on man, nor to restrict and control him. On the contrary, they were given out of His mercy and boundless love for the one He had created in His image and likeness. It was His will that man too should be motivated in all his relations by mercy and love. And, even though His people often received His law as restrictions on their freedom—an oppressive code of "do's and don'ts"—He gave them so that they might learn to love Him and their fellow man.

God is love (1 Jn 4:8), and His love is at work in all that He does and has done for man, in the creation, in His providential care and in the redemption. "What is man, that thou..shouldest set thine heart upon him?" (Job 7:17). "For God so loved the world..." (Jn 3:16). Love is the underlying principle of all the commandments. When He was asked which was the "great commandment in the law," Jesus answered: "Thou shalt love the Lord thy God with all thy heart, and with all thy soul, and with all thy mind. This is the first and great commandment. And the second is like unto it; Thou shalt love thy neighbor as thyself. On these two commandments hang all the law and the prophets" (Mt 22:36-40: Lk 10:26-27). But this was not a new concept introduced by Jesus, but was always the spirit of the commandments even under the old Covenant (see Dt 6:5 and Lev 19:18). On the other hand, the Lord did add a new dimension to the commandments: "A new commandment I give unto you, That ye love one another; as I have loved you, that ye also love one another. By this shall all know that ye are my disciples, if ye have love one to another" (Jn 13:34-35). The newness of this commandment is the expressed will of the Son of God that we love one another as He has loved us—that is, with a self-giving, selfless, sacrificial love. This He commanded His disciples after He had told them of His death on behalf of mankind.

Now, as the Lord begins to demonstrate how the commandments are to be understood and kept by His disciples, He chooses to introduce each example by such expressions as: "Ye have heard that it was said to them of old time..." (Note that it is "to them" and not "by them" as some translations put it.) The Son of God is the Law-giver, and it was He who revealed God's will to Moses in the first place, but He prefers to refer to the giving of the commandments in the passive, "it was said." St John Chrysostom thinks that if He had said, "I said to them of old time," He would have made it more difficult for His hearers to appreciate His message, since they might have been more concerned with His identifying Himself as the Divine Legislator, which fact is not His point just now. If He had said, "My Father said to them of old time," He might have appeared to be contrasting the Father's will with His. The point of His emphasis here is that it was time for the full implications of the commandments and the motive for their being given to be understood. He is saying too that far more will be expected of God's people under the New Covenant than under the old (Homily XVI, *On Matthew*).

When we understand that God provided the commandments as guides in the way of love, we can appreciate why He begins His explanation of their true meaning with the Sixth Commandment, "Thou shalt not kill." Murder is the consequence of the very opposite of love—hatred, which has no place in the life of one who follows Christ. The Lord's preaching, throughout His earthly life, will emphasize this truth over and over again. Later, St John the apostle will be able to write a kind of summary of the Lord's teaching about love (1 Jn 3 and 4): "Let us love one another: for love is of God: and everyone that loveth is born of God, and knoweth God. He that loveth not knoweth not God; for God is love." He that falls into hatred, then, violates the Sixth Commandment: "whosoever hateth his brother is a murderer; and ye know that no murderer hath eternal life abiding in him" (1 Jn 3:15).

Just as our Lord characteristically introduced the examples of His "new" law with "Ye have heard that it was said to them of old time," He also begins His explanation of each with "But I say unto you." St John Chrysostom's commentary on these passages contains this note:

> Do you see authority in perfection? Do you see a bearing suited to a legislator? Why, which among the prophets ever spoke like this? which among righteous men? which among the patriarchs? None: but, they said, "Thus saith the Lord." But the Son not so. Because they were publishing their Master's commands, He, His Father's. And when I say, "His Father's," I mean His own. "For mine" says He, "are thine, and thine are mine." (Jn 17:10). And they had their fellow-servants to legislate for, He His own servants (Homily XVI, *On Matthew*).

CHAPTER 11

When our Lord Jesus Christ had revealed his relation to the Law and the prophets, He solemnly warned his followers: "Except your righteousness shall exceed the righteousness of the scribes and Pharisees, ye shall in no case enter into the kingdom of heaven" (Mt 6:20). Righteousness as the aim of the life of the religious man was something familiar to the disciples as it was to all Jews: it was referred to throughout the Old Testament, and was understood as "the right conduct of man, the rectitude or uprightness of his life, in accordance with the will of God." It apparently had become common, however, among the Jews for righteousness to mean simply literal obedience to the law, and for persons who did not openly transgress any of the commandments to be counted as righteous. The real intent of the law was either misunderstood or distorted: "For they (the Jews) being ignorant of God's righteousness, and going about to establish their own righteousness, have not submitted themselves to the righteousness of God" (Rom 10:3).

When the Lord says, "Ye have heard...But I say unto you..." He announces that He is about to describe God's righteousness, the righteousness expected of His followers. His procedure is to state the law or commandment in its simplest form, without any hint of doing away with it, and then to go behind the law and show His (that is, the Lawgiver's) concern for what is in the heart of man, for his spiritual state. Here, He fulfills the prophecies concerning the new law and the new covenant:

> Behold, the days come, saith the Lord, that I will make a new covenant with the house of Israel, and with the house of Judah...After these days...I will put my law in their inward parts, and write it in their hearts... (Jer 31:31, 33)

> I will give them one heart, and I will put a new spirit within you; and I will take the stony heart out of their flesh, and will give a heart of flesh; that they may walk in my statutes, and keep mine ordinances, and do them; and they shall be my people and I shall be their God" (Ezek 11:19-20).

The first commandment that the Lord explains is the sixth (of the Ten): "Ye have heard that it was said to them of old time, Thou shalt not kill; and whosoever shall kill shall be in danger of the judgment" (Mt 5:21). He no doubt begins here because killing and its causes are the direct denial of love, the underlying principle of all God's commandments to men.

Hatred is the opposite of love and is a form of murder, as St John tells us (1 Jn 3:15). Hatred may be personal, but it can also be impersonal: some people hate people they do not even know; some even wish the death of a stranger. Whatever form it takes, hatred reveals a total lack of love, a lack of respect for a fellow human being, and a rejection of the essential idea that we are all created in the image of God.

But the Lord goes further than the immediate cause of murder: He is concerned with the "motive of the motive," and He tells us that what lies behind hatred is anger: "Whosoever is angry with his brother (without a cause) shall be in danger of the judgment" (Mt 5:22). Anger may or may not manifest itself openly. One may be so angry with another that all relations with him are cut off, thus, mentally removing him from existence, murdering him spiritually.

Anger may also end up in another type of murder—character assassination. The three cases in the Lord's illustration are something like a parable, each state of mind and its accompanying action giving way predictably to the next. Each is a degree in the process: anger first, calling someone by a name that shows contempt, and finally calling someone by a name equals a curse. The terms used are somewhat relative, but the Lord's meaning is precise. We might paraphrase the three degrees of anger's manifestation in this way: If anger deserves the judgment of the judges of society, and if calling someone an imbecile or stupid calls for the judgment of the spiritual leaders, then taking away a person's worth, degrading him, incurs the judgment of God. "Whosoever is angry...and whosoever shall say to his brother, Raca, shall be in danger of the council; but whosoever shall say, Thou fool, shall be danger of hell fire" (v. 22).

The Jews were accustomed to bring offerings for the forgiveness of sins to the temple in Jerusalem. Using this custom as an example, the Lord tells his disciples what the spirit of offering and worship must be: the gifts are unacceptable to God if the offerer holds anything in his heart against anyone. We must not withhold forgiveness, keep resentment in our hearts, or hold grudges, even when the other person is clearly at fault.

Reconciliation is Christ's way: just as He reconciled man to God in Himself, although it was man who separated himself, so also He commands us to be reconciled to one another. "Therefore if thou bring thy gift to the altar, and there rememberest that thy brother hath ought against thee; leave there thy gift before the altar, and go thy way; first be reconciled to thy brother, and then come and offer thy gift" (vv. 23-24).

The last two verses of this section (vv. 25-26) have to do with the application of the principle of forgiveness and reconciliation in this world, but they also tell us something important about the consequences of the failure to be reconciled for a person's spiritual state:

> Agree with thine adversary quickly, whilst thou art in the way with him; lest at any time the adversary deliver thee to the judge, and the judge deliver thee to the officer, and thou be cast into prison. Verily I say unto thee, thou shalt by no means come out thence, till thou has paid the uttermost farthing.

Perhaps a more literal translation of some of the vocabulary of these verses will make it easier to understand the Lord's meaning here. "Agree" (*evnoon* in Greek means "be well disposed"); "adversary" (*antidikos*) is usually an accuser, one who accuses another of a wrong. We should hasten to come to an understanding with such an accuser, even when a court case is imminent ("whilst thou art in the way with him"). This act could prevent all the disagreeable consequences of going to court (being delivered to the judge, to the bailiff, and finally to jail). Literally, one has to avoid spending time in prison if possible, but this is the prison of one's conscience; that is, the conscience of a person who has made no attempt at settling a matter in a peaceable way is a prison from which it is hard to get release. However, as true as all this may be, the same principle of reconciliation, forgiveness and love is at the heart of this example, and it is God's judgment that must be our ultimate concern.

Chapter 12

In Psalm 50(51), David prays: "Create in me a clean heart, O God, and renew a right spirit within me" (v.11). At the beginning of the Sermon of the Mount, our Lord declares "the clean of heart" to be blessed. When He reveals the true spirit of God's commandments, one of the most important meanings of that cleanness or purity of heart becomes clear.

> Ye have heard that it was said to them of old time.
> Thou shalt not commit adultery; but I say unto you,
> that whosoever looketh on a woman to lust after her
> hath committed adultery with her already in his heart
> (vv. 27-29).

Just as He had shown us that there is more than one way to murder, that the anger in a person's heart can become spiritual murder, He goes on now to the second of the commandments that were designed to instill love in the hearts of men and women, and not to restrict their freedom. Again, He goes behind the simple commandment, "Thou shalt not commit adultery," to attack the very impurity that finally manifests itself in an act. To be sure, the commandment remains in force, but He teaches us that the basic wrong lies in the spirit of selfishness and gratification that distorts the sex act and separates it from love.

The two emotions, anger and desire, which are the causes of so much evil and which so many people think are perfectly natural and therefore not wrong in themselves, can be transformed and come under the domination of the spirit according to God's will. But we must understand that it is not simply by deciding that a person can accomplish this transformation. It is rather by perceiving first that it is God's will for man that he keep himself free from evil. Then, becoming a child of the kingdom, of God's reign, he may be freed by the power of the Holy Spirit from the very things that enslave him and make him a child of the reign of this world.

The Lord again teaches us that an external compliance with the law is not what is required of His followers, but rather a conversion that eliminates the very desire behind the violation of the law. He rejects the attempts of some to justify themselves, those who think that it does not matter what is in the heart, as long as it does not become action, or that they are not just as responsible for their impure thoughts.

The Lord summarizes the harm involved in sexual preoccupation with the expression, "whosoever looketh on a woman to lust after her hath committed adultery with her already in his heart." And the Fathers of the Church (St John Chrysostom, St Ambrose and St Augustine, among others) explore the many ways in which one may "look to lust." Sometimes, the whole thing remains entirely in the mind, either as a memory or some imagined act. In an unchaste mind, it may reach the point of being involuntary and appear to be provoked, but such a mind is already under the control of the Evil One, who constantly provokes man and desires to enslave him. It is not uncommon for some to excite themselves by looking at drawings, photographs and even movies, reasoning within themselves that they still are not guilty as long as they do not put their thoughts into practice. But this kind of autoeroticism is not only sinful and a violation of Christ's will that we not "look to lust"; but it is a sure way to weaken ourselves spiritually and kill our spirit.

> And if thy right eye offend thee, pluck it out, and cast it from thee: for it is profitable for thee that one of thy members should perish, and not that thy whole body should be cast into hell. And if thy right hand offend thee, cut it off, and cast it from thee; for it is profitable for thee that one of thy members should perish, and not that thy whole body should be cast into hell (vv. 29-30).

The Lord forbids "looking on a woman to lust after her," Now he continues (with a metaphor, according to St John Chrysostom) probing the causes of impurity of heart, and the eye is obviously the body member involved in the "look." The body or the flesh, however, is not what is to blame; there is something else behind the flesh: the mind, the spirit and the will. Obviously, being blinded in one eye will not make the heart pure. There are situations and persons that provide the occasion for sin, whether in thought, word or deed. The Fathers assure us that here the Lord is commanding us to rid ourselves of the occasion for sin rather than to mutilate ourselves.

Let us pay attention to what St John Chrysostom says about this (Homily 17, *On Matthew*): "Again, had He been speaking of members of the body, He would not have said it of one eye, not of the right eye only, but of both. For he who is offended by his right eye, most evidently will incur the same evil by his left also. Why then did He mention the right eye, and add the hand? To show you that not of limbs is He speaking, but of them that are near unto us. Thus, 'If,' says He, 'you should love any one as though he were instead of a right eye; If you think him so profitable to you as to esteem him in the place of a hand, and he hurts your soul; these you must cut off;' And note the emphasis; for He does not say, 'Withdraw from him,' but to show the fullness of the separation, 'pluck it out and cast it from thee.'" Again, it is from the very situations and people that provoke us to sin that we must separate ourselves. On the other hand, the one who provokes may do so unintentionally. If this is so, then the separation will be beneficial to both parties. If, however, his provocation is intentional, you will benefit him by putting an end to his attempt to offend you. Finally, the Lord shows his love for all men and His will that they love one another by these commandments. This is the very basis of the new, authentic life of man revealed to us in His becoming man, revealing to us directly what man is to be.

CHAPTER 13

*It hath been said, Whosoever shall put away his wife,
let him give her a writing of divorcement: But I say
unto you, that whosoever shall put away his wife
saving for the cause of fornication, causeth her to
commit adultery: and whosoever shall marry her that
is divorced committeth adultery* (Mt 5:31-32).

The Lord's reference, "It has been said, whosoever shall put
away his wife..." is to Deuteronomy 24:14, in which it
appears that God's original commandment is quite liberal: a
practice like the modern one of getting rid of a husband or
wife that one is not pleased with seems to have been approved.
Later, when the Pharisees questioned His teachings, Jesus
explained the apparent inconsistency in the revelation of
God's will in these terms: "Moses because of the hardness of
your hearts suffered you to put away your wives: but from the
beginning it was not so" (Mt 19:8).

St John Chrysostom reminds us that the "bill of divorcement" law was not a primary law, but that it has
been given to God's people to prevent even greater sins.
(See his Homily 17, *On Matthew*.) The last part of the
above cited verse is very significant: "from the beginning
it was not so." A number of the Fathers of the Church
were of the opinion that the morality of the period of the
Patriarchs was far higher than that of the period that
followed the escape of Israel from Egypt. (See St Augustine, *First Catechetical Instruction*, 19-33; and especially
St Justin Martyr, *Dialogue with Trypho*, Chapters 19-21,
where he shows that because Jews turned away from God,
certain things were instituted, such as circumcision and

the Sabbath, to make them remember Him and His pact
with them. They point out that Noah and Melchizedek
were not circumcised nor did they observe the Sabbath,
yet they pleased God. The same is said of the relaxation
of the fundamental laws of human conduct.) Moses often
had to plead with God to lighten the burden of a strict
following of His commandments because of the perver-
sity of the people of Israel. Some of the Fathers saw in
Christ's teachings a restoration of the call to holiness and
purity of the people before the Exodus.

God's commandments, restated and strengthened in
the teachings of Christ, seem at first to be addressed
solely to the male. Perhaps His reason for doing this was
the predisposition of His hearers, who were familiar with
the law and of the secondary place seemingly accorded to
women, and might not have understood His radical depar-
ture from their traditional comprehension of it. He undoubtedly approached His teachings concerning the law
in such a way as to establish first His identity as the
original Lawgiver. As He continues to reveal God's
moral demands on the human race, it will be shown that
men and women have an equal dignity and equal responsibility before God for their behavior. He is much stricter
in His teachings about divorce and the adultery that re-
sults from it, when He declares without qualification
"Whosoever putteth away his wife, and marrieth another,
committeth adultery: and whosoever marrieth her that is
put away from her husband committeth adultery" (Lk
16:18). In other words, it is not simply that the husband
causes his wife that is put away to commit adultery, but
he also, if he remarries, commits adultery. The same
applies to the woman who initiates the break (Mk 10:12).

Still, He has allowed a motive for divorce—fornication or infidelity. Such an illicit relation has already caused a rupture of the marriage. The "hardness of heart" attributed to the Jews is not absent from those among the "new Jews," that is, the Christian people; and the Church, with its authority to loose and to bind given to it directly by Christ, does allow some divorces and even remarriages, but always when some form of infidelity is involved.

St John Chrysostom sounds a warning to those of legalistic mind, who might find for themselves a justification for divorce on any other grounds: "Therefore, you see, after this He presses the point without reserve, and builds up this fear as a bulwark, urging on the husband the great danger, if he does cast her out, in that he makes himself accountable for her adultery. Thus, lest you being told, 'pluck out the eye,' should suppose this to be said even of a wife: He added in good time this corrective, in one way only giving leave to cast her out, but no otherwise" (*Op. Cit*).

Once again, we see in this aspect of the teachings of Christ the underlying motivation for all human relationships—love. Conversion to Christ and His way must bring an end to "hardness of heart," for conversion means precisely a change of heart. Marriage is to be understood as a divine institution in which a man and a woman have the greatest possibility for love and unselfish giving. It is of the nature of the children of the Kingdom to reflect God's love in all relationships, but especially in the union of marriage. Those whom the Lord calls blessed at the beginning of the "Sermon" are no longer capable of the self-indulgence and self-centeredness that are the basic

motives behind divorce. "For he that is meek, and a
peacemaker, and poor in spirit, and merciful, how shall
he cast out his wife? He that is used to reconcile others,
how shall he be at variance with her that is his own?"
(St John Chrysostom, *Op. Cit.*)

Chapter 14

*Again, ye have heard that it hath been said to them of
old time, Thou shalt not forswear thyself, but shalt
perform unto the Lord thine oaths: but I say unto you,
Swear not at all; neither by heaven, for it is God's
throne; nor by the earth; for it is His footstool; neither by Jerusalem; for it is the city of the Great King.
Neither shalt thou swear by thy head, because thou
canst not make one hair white or black, but let your
communication be, Yea, yea; Nay, nay; for whatsoever is more than these cometh of evil* (Mt 5:33-37).

The principle to which the Lord refers in these lines had
always been taken seriously by most of the Hebrew people. It was taken for granted that one would keep his promise.
It was unthinkable to swear falsely or perjure oneself in God's
name (Lev 19:12). That was, after all, what the commandment, "Thou shalt not take the name of the Lord thy God in
vain," was all about, although it includes the impious practice
of using God's name frivolously or blasphemously. "If a man
vow a vow unto the Lord, or swear an oath to bind his soul
with a bond; he shall not break his word..." (Num 30:2).
"When thou shalt vow a vow unto the Lord thy God, thou shalt
not slack to pay it; for the Lord thy God will surely require it
of thee; and it would be sin in thee" (Dt 23:21).

The practice of making such vows or taking such oaths was, in Mosaic Law, not only allowed, but even sanctioned. Therefore, when Jesus declared, "But I say unto you, swear not at all," the apparent contradiction must have startled the disciples. After all, He had given them to understand that He was completing and perfecting a law that He had given in the first place.

The Fathers (and particularly St John Chrysostom, to whom we often turn for explanations of Scripture) find in these verses a precise example of the Lord's perfecting of His own law. The purpose of the old law, they say, was to prepare the people for the new law; the first and most important step in that process was to lead them away from idolatry. We recall that the Hebrews who had been liberated from Egypt by the direct intervention of God fell into idolatry: "And the children of Israel did evil in the sight of the Lord, and served Baalim...and followed other gods, of the gods of the people round about them..." (Jg 2:11-12). "And indeed this very thing, the oath was ordained of old for this cause, that they might not swear by the idols" (St John Chrysostom, Homily 17, *On Matthew*). So, the oath commanded by God was preliminary to the prohibition of the oath altogether, at a later time, when the principle of service to the one God had been well established. In these teachings, the Lord shows His disciples what He meant by "their righteousness having to exceed that of the scribes and Pharisees" (Mt 5:20).

The new commandment, "Swear not at all," must be understood in the light of that new righteousness, not just as an additional stricter law. The whole series of qualities that make man blessed—the poor in spirit, the merciful, the clean of heart, etc.—are signs of a whole new style of life. Thus, a person who lives righteously according to this revelation of God's will, will not have need of any oath—his life and the truth by which he lives are his witnesses. If he makes a promise, he keeps it; if he declares something to be true, his character is such that he is not suspected of lying. If he says "yes" he means "yes" and if "no, no." These passages reveal the infinite wisdom of God in preparing one particular people for the final revelation of His righteousness, so that, through them, the whole world and all people might be brought to a knowledge of Him. That revelation is exactly what we see in the words and works of Jesus Christ.

Since the Pharisees regarded as binding an oath made in the name of God, they sought to keep the "letter of the law" by swearing by heaven, the earth, Jerusalem, or even by one's own head, so as to make the oath not absolutely binding. Jesus specifically forbids this legalistic and evasive kind of swearing, for heaven is His throne, the earth is His footstool, Jerusalem is His city, and one cannot change the nature even of the hair of his head. The point is that everything is not only God's creation but He has dominion over all things, and since He is present everywhere, all oaths and promises are, in effect, made in His name and in His presence.

When He says, "Whatsoever is more than 'yea' or 'nay' cometh from evil" (that is, from the evil one), He points to the fact that the presence and influence of the devil in human life and society, constantly at work against God, cause distrust among men and women. Christians themselves are sometimes guilty of succumbing to his influence and sometimes they are simply victims of it. They, as members of a secular society, are required to "render unto Caesar" in taking judicial oaths, oaths of allegiance, etc. In so doing, they participate, in a sense, in this world's evil. They must not accept freely and gladly this behavior which is inconsistent with God's will for them, any more than they can accept their having to go to war for their country. A Christian, one who seeks God's righteousness, must be aware of this and repent of it, even when it is not his fault.

The Christian life, as our Lord teaches us, is one in which truth is both sought and practiced. Along with truth, we may mention sincerity, dependability and integrity. A Christian's language should be free of foolishness, frivolity and insincerity. He must break himself of swearing, even if it is a little habit to which he attaches no importance. Again, God's will for His people is that they live entirely in accordance with the righteousness He reveals in Jesus Christ, that they lie not and do the truth, have fellowship with Him and walk in the light (see 1 Jn 1:6).

CHAPTER 15

The Fathers of the Church in general see the revelation of God's will for man as a progressive thing. For them, what some people take as an inconsistency between the Law and Christ's moral teachings, between the "Ye have heard that it was said to them of old time," and the "But I say unto you," is only apparent. They insist on the plan whereby God prepared the Hebrews for His final revelation, a plan that, given man's fallen condition, necessarily called for a step-by-step development. They were aware that the inability of some to reconcile the Old Covenant with the New had led to their rejection of the former; for example, the Marcionites and later the Manicheans. They had an answer for those who could not see how the same divine Lawgiver could command the so-called law of retaliation (Lev 24:17-20), to which our Lord refers in Matthew 5:38, and His law of non-resistance to evil. He says: "Ye have heard that it hath been said, An eye for an eye, and a tooth for a tooth: But I say unto you, that ye resist not evil: but whosoever shall smite thee on thy right cheek, turn to him the other also."

In the first place, the Fathers do not see that particular "old law" as simply giving a person who has been wronged the right to retaliate in kind, as much as they see it as a limitation on arbitrary vengeance. Without any doubt, from the very time the law was given there were among the Jews those who understood the real intention behind it: to prevent the injured party's avenging the wrong dealt him by inflicting an even greater injury on the offender. If we take the whole Old Testament into consideration, we find throughout the concept that vengeance belongs to God (see Dt 32:35, Ps 93[94] and Jer 20;12). Revenge was expressly forbidden: "Say not thou, I will recompense evil; but wait in the Lord, and He shall save thee" (Pr 20:22); "Say not, I will do so to him as he hath done to me: I will render unto the man according to his work" (Pr 24:29).

At the time of Christ, however, many Jews had come to take the laws in isolation from their context and considered that retaliation was a sacred, God-given right. It is interesting to note that later on the Moslems, who appropriated much of the Old Testament for their sacred book, the *Koran*, did not understand the true spirit of the law given to God's people and, rejecting Christ's revelation of its meaning, reiterated the law of retaliation in a very uncompromising way.

We must always remember in our attempts to understand the true meaning of the Lord's teachings that He had set out to preach the Gospel of the Kingdom, to reveal the norms of behavior for those who would belong to the Kingdom of God, and to proclaim God's righteousness. He told His disciples, early in his "Sermon on the Mount," that if their righteousness did not exceed that of the scribes and the Pharisees, they could not enter the Kingdom (5:20). Their righteousness justified repaying what had been done, and only that, not going beyond it in retaliation. This law, given as an intermediate and temporary step, had been designed to prepare man for, and then to give way to, a higher law. In the light of this principle, Jesus' declared purpose—not to destroy the law, but to fulfill or perfect it—becomes clearer and clearer.

The Christian, then, will exceed the lesser righteousness of the Pharisee in that he will not only "not return evil for evil," but rather will even be ready to accept, for the Kingdom of heaven's sake, a further injury. This is one of the essential elements of the perfection that the Lord demands of us, and it is no surprise that He sums up all His teaching about the Law with: "Be ye therefore perfect as your Father which is in heaven is perfect" (5:48). This demand is, from a purely human viewpoint, impossible to fulfill. On the other hand, we receive it from Him who not only commanded it, but lived it, and has given us the grace to be transformed into His image. The supreme application of this principle which the Lord gives us is expressed in His own words from the Cross: "Father, forgive them, for they know not what they do" (Lk 23:34).

In verse 39, "But I say unto you, that ye resist not evil," St John Chrysostom says that "evil" (*to ponero*, in Greek) really means "the evil one," the devil. In other words, we must see in the unjust acts and the injuries done to us by others the work of the devil himself. So it is not just a general or abstract "evil" but the devil himself that we are told "not to resist." To be sure, He would have us resist the devil but not by "fighting fire with fire." Retaliation against an offending brother would not only be meaningless, it would be worse; for the devil, who sets brother against brother, will be happy to see us trying to even things up by avenging ourselves. Real resistance to the evil one consists of returning good for evil, putting a stop to the anger that has caused the injury in the first place with the only weapon the devil cannot resist—love.

While the Fathers make it clear that, just as in the Lord's own life, the possibility of our having to forgive someone who intentionally wrongs us is always present, they also think it far more likely that we may be called upon to apply this principle in another way. St Augustine, for example, gives us this very practical application:

> As regards compassion, they who feel it most minister to those whom they greatly love as if they were their own children, or some very dear friend in sickness, or little children, or insane persons, at whose hands they often endure many things; and if their welfare demand it, they even show themselves ready to endure more, until the weakness either of age or of disease pass away. And so, as regards those whom the Lord, the physician of souls, was instructing to take care of their neighbors, what else could He teach them, than that they endure quietly the infirmi-

ties of those whose welfare they wish to promote?
(*Our Lord's Sermon on the Mount*, xix, 57)

Here, as in all the "new" commandments Jesus has given thus far, we discover His underlying principle—love. Law is given in order that man might learn love. Later, He will summarize the Law, in response to the question, "Which is the great commandment in the Law?" by declaring that the first and great commandment is to love God, and the second is to love one's neighbor as oneself (Mt 22:36-39). The supreme act of love is to love your enemy, loving so deeply that you do good to those who do you evil.

CHAPTER 16

As we have seen, our Lord repudiates the law of "an eye for an eye, and a tooth for a tooth," and even requires of His followers the disposition to accept further insult and injury: "Whosoever shall smite thee on thy right cheek, turn to him the other also" (Mt 5:39). In addition, He demands a kind of self-denial that most people, even Christians, consider impractical. The modern Christian will probably dismiss the examples of verses 40 and 41 as perhaps applicable to Jesus' times, but not at all to the complex social situations of his own times. Yet the commandment stands: the "seeker after God's righteousness" must be willing to give more than he is compelled to give.

The two situations (being sued "at the law" and being compelled "to go a mile") are not at all farfetched or improbable. The likelihood of the average person's being involved in a lawsuit is greater at the present time than ever before, and it may simply be impossible to avoid some kind of self-defense. The intricacy of modern law (with all its loopholes in which the very idea of right and wrong is lost, the greed of some lawyers who provoke people to sue, and a sometimes exaggerated zeal for protecting the rights of criminals) makes the judicial system less and less capable of rendering just decisions. Still, a Christian stance consistent with our Lord's teachings in the face of such distortions of justice is what concerns us here. In verse 25, we are told to agree with our adversary (to be "kindly disposed" toward our accuser). This involves not only the willingness to come to an understanding with him, but an active attempt to do so; it also reminds us that even in these adverse circumstances, Christ's law of love and forgiveness must dominate our thinking and our reaction. Further, we must reject any temptation to take more than is due us, even when we could get away with it legally. In such "out of court" approaches to legal problems, we should think not just of our own profit or advantage, but also be concerned about the "adversary's" welfare.

The matter of being compelled to go a mile and the Lord's command to go two miles rather than the one may refer specifically to the right of the Roman legionnaire to commandeer workers from among noncitizens. It is not, however, without application to situations in our own contemporary life. How often are we compelled, because of a variety of relationships, to do something for someone? How often do we respond to these circumstances grudgingly and resentfully? Here we have a wonderful opportunity to teach ourselves a valuable lesson, to become more patient and generous, if only we will do more than we are obliged to do—in other words, go the second mile.

The Lord's demand in verse 42 ("Give to him that asketh of thee, and from him that would borrow of thee turn not thou away") is far less severe, and, indeed, is far easier to comply with. This is something that happens to most of us almost daily. Yet, because of its frequency, we often lose our patience and forget that the Lord still expects us to follow not only His commandment but likewise His example.

We have referred above to the "adversary's" welfare and our need to care about it. The Fathers stress a twofold benefit to be derived from a faithful following of these commandments of Christ. First, we benefit ourselves spiritually by learning to be patient, merciful and forgiving. Then, by example, we benefit the other person, who perhaps will be astounded, deeply impressed and even converted to Christ's way by our "unusual" behavior, by our unwillingness to answer violence with violence, to "fight fire with fire." (See St John Chrysostom, *On Matthew*, Homily 18.)

The rest of this portion of the Lord's Sermon on the Mount (that is, the rest of Chapter 5 of Matthew's Gospel) is devoted to love—the virtue that must take hold of us in all our day to day dealings with others.

Hatred of God's enemies by the people of God, although not specifically endorsed or commanded, seems to have been taken for granted (see Ps 139:19-22 and 140:9-11), and in Jesus' time apparently included those who had another religion and people of other nationalities or races. It goes without saying that this type of hatred not only exists today, but is cultivated. He, however, gives us no excuse for hating anyone, whether the enemy is personal or simply a person of another race, creed or nationality. "Love your enemies, bless them that curse you, do good to them that hate you, and pray for them which despitefully use you, and persecute you" (verse 44). These words need no further explanation or elaboration.

The aim of life in Christ given by the power of the Holy Spirit is to become children of the heavenly Father, to become citizens of the Kingdom of Heaven. The path that leads to the Kingdom is the path of love and forgiveness, as almost everything that Christ says in this sermon emphasizes. He has a will for those who would follow Him: He sets the standards of human behavior, not because they are logical or reasonable, but precisely because they are His will for us. No greater reason can be offered for being good to our enemies, adversaries, opponents or rivals and loving them than this: "Your Father...maketh His sun to rise on the evil and on the good, and sendeth rain on the just and on the unjust" (verse 45). Even the worst of men and women love their own families and their own kind. The one who would be truly a child of the Kingdom will love all without distinction. Sometimes this high regard for all manifests itself in a simple greeting, in not ignoring someone—in short, in remembering another's dignity as a child of God. It is completely unbecoming for a Christian to refuse to speak to someone— even the worst sinner greets his own brothers.

The chapter ends with the familiar verse, "Be ye perfect, even as your Father which is in heaven is perfect" (verse 46). God's perfection has been demonstrated to us in His love for us: "In this was manifested the love of God toward us, because God sent His only begotten Son into the world, that we might live through Him" (1 Jn 4:9). "But God commendeth His love toward us, in that, while we were yet sinners, Christ died for us" (Rom 5:8). The Sermon on the Mount shows us that the way to perfection is the way of love, of God and of our fellow man.

III

The New Life in Christ

CHAPTER 17

In the first part of the Sermon of the Mount (Matthew, Chapter 5), the Lord, after proclaiming that the kingdom of God is at hand, tells His disciples of the nature of the conversion that makes them children of the kingdom. Since the kingdom refers not only to the future reign of God in the world to come but also to His present reign in men's hearts, Jesus teaches them how to "seek first the kingdom of God and His righteousness" (Mt 6:33). Because, in St Paul's words, men "being ignorant of God's righteousness, and going about to establish their own righteousness, have not submitted themselves unto the righteousness of God" (Rom 10:3), it was the Lord's purpose to declare exactly what God's righteousness is, in opposition to the righteousness of men.

We find the Lord, in Chapter 6, describing how belonging to the kingdom of God will affect the whole of a person's life. There is not one single aspect of life that can be left unchanged or unconverted by the direct revelation of God's will and His demands on man which Jesus teaches. And it is with the religious life that He begins.

The three basic acts of piety among the Jews, ever since God had made His pact with them, were almsgiving, prayer and fasting. The godly man was one who gave alms, prayed and fasted. The disciples of Christ no doubt took for granted the fact that they too would give alms, pray and fast, since He had not come to destroy the law and the prophets, but to fulfill them. By dealing with these things first, He confirms that these three things would still be foremost among the forms of service and worship that the children of the kingdom would follow.

St John Chrysostom (Homily 19, *On Matthew*) says this:

> Christ roots out in the remainder of the Sermon the most tyrannical passion of all, the rage and madness with respect to vainglory, which springs up in them that do right. But after He had led them on to self-command, then He proceeds to purge away the alloy (that which adulterates or spoils) which secretly subsists with it.

The greatest temptation that arises to mar one's resolve to do God's will, the weapon the devil most often uses to destroy man's best intentions, is the desire to be recognized and praised by others. Even when a person is motivated by a real feeling of compassion, he often finds himself not wanting his good deeds to go unnoticed. Sometimes charitable deeds are done for the wrong reason altogether: to be known as a philanthropist. When we hear that the Lord says in Matthew 6:1, "Take heed that ye do not your alms before men, to be seen of them, otherwise ye have no reward of your Father which is in heaven," we understand that He is condemning those things that are done for show, because they are really not done for others, but for oneself. How often we see the philanthropists of our time photographed handing a check to the representative of some social agency, or worse, giving a basket of food to some needy person at Thanksgiving or Christmas.

Surely this is what the Lord means when He says, "do not sound a trumpet before thee, as the hypocrites do in the synagogues and in the streets, that they may have the glory of men." He calls these charitable individuals "hypocrites"—a word that originally meant "actor." And the word translated "to be seen," *theatinai*, is to be seen as in a theater, *theatron*.

One might object that it is not always possible to do a good deed without being seen, at least by the one who benefits from an act of generosity. But it is the intention that the Lord speaks of: the *pros* before the verb means "in order to" or "for the purpose of." So the conclusion is that those who do their acts of almsgiving in order to be seen and praised by others, "have their reward." They get what they wanted, and that is all they get: "Ye have no reward of your Father which is in heaven."

Genuine righteousness even tries to evade itself. When the Lord says in verse 3, "When thou doest thine alms, let not thy left hand know what thy right hand doeth," He no doubt means that the truly righteous person—one who has been truly converted to His way—does his good deed spontaneously, responds readily to needs, does not even think of himself as doing a good deed, and is probably surprised if he is praised and thanked for it.

"That thine alms may be in secret: and thy Father which seeth in secret himself shall reward thee openly." God is everywhere present and knows not only every deed that is done but also the intention or motivation behind it. There will indeed be a reward for true righteousness, and that reward will be given openly, but not in this life. Even if our deeds are hidden from others in this world, when all are called before the dread judgment seat of Christ, they will be revealed.

CHAPTER 18

And when thou prayest, thou shalt not be as the hypocrites are: for they love to pray standing in the synagogues and in the corners of the streets, that they

may be seen of men. Verily I say unto you, They have
their reward (Mt 6:5).

The Lord thus continues to teach His disciples concerning
the practice of the Christian life. Just as He had begun this
part of the Sermon with instructions on the spirit of almsgiving, on what true charity is, He now tells them about what it
is to pray. Again, He says, "When thou prayest..." as He has
said, "When thou doest alms...," and as He will say, "When
ye fast...," showing in this way that the three basic acts of piety
practiced by the Jews will also be practiced by His followers.

Apparently there have always been religious people
who have wanted to impress others with their devoutness.
Things have not changed much: just as there are some
"almsgivers" who will give only if they are seen by
others, there are also those who want to be known as men
of prayer. They contrive to have others observe them in
deep devotion. They clasp their hands, beat their breasts,
and cast their eyes heavenward. They make deeper bows
than anyone else. (All of these gestures are good and
natural to the praying person, if his only wish is to pray,
to worship and to praise God.) They often have the admiration of those who see them, and when the Lord says,
"They have their reward," He means that the admiration
is the extent of their reward.

We must pray, always conscious of our unworthiness,
with contrition, with inward tears, but we must not think
that there is anything wrong if the pain we feel inwardly
is expressed outwardly as well. What is wrong is an
outward expression with no inward feeling. The words of
the Lord given to the Prophet Joel for the Hebrews testify
to the fact that even under the Old Covenant the spirit of
true prayer was the same:

> Therefore also now, saith the Lord, turn ye unto me with all your heart, and with fasting, and with weeping and with mourning. And rend your hearts, not your garments... (Jl 2:12-13).

> But thou when thou prayest, enter into thy closet, and when thou hast shut thy door, pray to thy Father which is in secret; and thy Father which seeth in secret shall reward thee openly (v.6).

Does this mean that we should always pray alone and not in company with others? What about the common prayer of the Church? After all, many of the prayers in the services are in the plural: "We pray thee," "We ask thee," "We praise thee," etc. And then the Lord Himself says later: "For where two or three are gathered together in my name" (specifically for prayer, according to the preceding verse), "there am I in the midst of them" (Mt 18:20). Obviously Christ's disciples and His followers are to pray together. There are places in the Gospels in which He shows that it is His will. On the other hand, it is in the same spirit of devotion to God and not in order to impress others that we pray, either alone or with others. St John Chrysostom says:

> Since even if you should enter into your closet, and having shut the door, should do it for display, the doors will do you no good...He desires you...even to shut the doors of the mind...and if we who pray and beseech do not pay attention to what we are doing, but rather are distracted and wander, how do we expect God to pay attention to us? (*On Matthew,* Homily 19)

> But when ye pray, use not vain repetitions, as the heathens do: for they think they shall be heard for their much speaking. Be not ye therefore like unto them: for your Father knoweth what things ye have need of, before ye ask Him (vv. 7-8).

Now the Lord has changed to the plural: where in verses 5 and 6, He had taught us using the singular "thou," He now uses the plural "ye." We may understand from this that He intends for us to pray together as well as in private. The expression, "use not vain repetitions," is a translation of the Greek *me battalogesete*, "babbling," "using empty words," or "frivolous talk." The heathen apparently prayed with formulas or magic phrases, which they either did not understand or simply repeated over and over without feeling anything of love or devotion. Christians could be in danger of using Christian prayers in the same way. Repetition is in itself of no value. The prayer that arises from the heart, even if repeated, is the prayer that reaches heaven. God is not moved to respond to our needs just because we shout them again and again, or because we recite automatically the right formula.

This last admonition also reveals the inappropriateness of selfish petitions, or such unsuitable requests as "kingdoms, and glory, and to get the better of enemies, and abundance of wealth, and in general what does not at all concern us." (St John Chrysostom, *ibid.*)

We pray because we have the need to speak to our Father, and, since He loves us, we love Him. We pray in order to give Him praise and to express our total dependence on Him. In prayer, we express our willingness to conform our lives and our use of the things He has given us to His will. We express our needs in prayer, not because He does not know what we need, but because we declare in the enumeration of them our humble willingness to be content with what He gives us. We are saying in effect, "we think we need these things, but if thou knowest that I need them not, I humbly accept thy will for me."

CHAPTER 19

A fter having taught the disciples the spirit of prayer, the Lord gives them the model prayer: "After this manner therefore pray ye"(Mt 6:6). Although Jesus did not direct them to use the exact words of this prayer exclusively, the Church from the beginning, receiving it as the most perfect of all prayers, has repeated it just as He gave it over and over again. It is used in the public prayer of the Church and in the personal prayers of all Christians.

St Luke records the prayer as a response to the disciples' earnest request, "Lord, teach us to pray" (Lk 11:11). In St Matthew's Gospel, it is a part of the Lord's teaching on prayer in the Sermon on the Mount.

"Our Father which art in heaven."

Using "our" the Lord again emphasizes a characteristic of Christian prayer: it is always with our brothers and sisters in mind that we pray, whether we pray alone or in the company of others. "Father" is a name that shows our relationship to God. He is one that is approached as a loving Father, and we address Him with love and confidence. When He adds, "which art in heaven," He tells us that in prayer we first lift our minds and our hearts from earthly concerns and fix our attention on Him as the divine and perfect one on whom we depend. There were many other times when Jesus mentioned His Father and used the same epithet, "which is in heaven."

"Hallowed be thy name."

Before anything else, as God's children, we ask that in us, in our life, our deeds, and even in our innermost thoughts, His name be glorified. In other words, our first petition in prayer is totally unselfish: that we may live in such a pure way that God may be glorified by other people. As St Paul was able to declare after his conversion and having preached the faith that he once sought to destroy, "They glorified God in me" (Gal 1:24).

"Thy kingdom come."

Next we declare the aim and goal of our own life as Christians: that the Kingdom of God be realized among us and in us even in this present life, since where love is, the kingdom is already present. This petition also expresses our longing for the Second Coming of Christ and for the final realization of the Kingdom of God in the world to come. "What manner of persons ought ye to be in all holy conversation and godliness, looking for and hastening unto the coming of the day of God" (2 Pet 3:12).

"Thy will be done in earth, as it is in heaven."

When we ask that the will of God be done on earth as it is in heaven, we ask that it be done first of all in us and by us. We must be obedient, ever seeking to understand what the will of the Lord is for us (Eph 5:17). It is also the proper concern of followers of Christ that God's will be done by others too. We not only lament that it is not, but even work to see that it is done. The angels and the saints in heaven follow His will and "do His commandments, hearkening unto the voice of His word" (Ps 102(103):20). This must also be our earnest desire.

"Give us this day our daily bread."

The first petition in which we ask for something for ourselves is a request for that thing which is most needed by us all: our daily bread. This bread, as the word of God teaches us, is understood in at least three ways. The very word "daily" is a translation of the Greek *epiousion*. This literally means "above essence," and some of the Fathers of the Church (such as St Cyril of Jerusalem) taught that this means the spiritual bread of the Eucharist, the most pure body of the Lord. He says of Himself: "I am the living bread which came down from heaven: if any man eat of this bread, he shall live forever: And the bread that I will give is my flesh" (Jn 6:51). Daily bread is also the word of God, which sustains every believer. "Man shall not live by bread alone, but by every word that proceedeth out of the mouth of God" (Mt 4:4).

Daily bread is likewise everything that is necessary for our life. Although God certainly knows our needs, we express both our humility and our dependence on Him by asking for them. It is also important for the Christian to realize that he must ask not for great wealth or for more than he needs. When he asks for bread, he must also be mindful of the needs of others, especially for those who truly are hungry and deprived of what they need.

"And forgive us our debts, as we forgive our debtors."

Again our requests must have to do with our spiritual life above all else, and nothing is more important in the life of a Christian than to be forgiven of his sins. "Debts" is used to refer to all kinds of transgressions, since the word itself implies obligations both to God and to our fellow man, debts of behavior and feeling that we have failed to pay. (If it be argued that in modern speech "debts" usually has to do with money, it could also be pointed out that "trespasses" usually means violations of property rights.) But, as we will be told by the Lord Himself a little farther on, we cannot expect to be forgiven if we ourselves are unwilling to forgive (Mt 6:14-15). Forgiveness is the very essence of the Christian life.

"And lead us not into temptation."

Some people have a lot of trouble with this petition, thinking that it implies that God Himself tempts us. St James the Apostle makes the meaning of this petition clear: "Blessed is the man that endureth temptation: for when he is tried, he shall receive the crown of life, which the Lord hath promised to them that love Him. Let no man say when he is tempted, I am tempted with evil, neither tempteth He any man: but every man is tempted, when he is drawn away of his own lust, and enticed" (Jas 1:12-14).

"But deliver us from evil."

The last petition of the prayer is for deliverance not only from evil but from the one who is the cause of it, the evil one, the devil. We declare our desire and intention to renounce evil and Satan, with the help of God. In the Lord's prayer (usually called the "high priestly prayer") before His crucifixion, He prays that all His disciples may be kept from the evil one (Jn 17:15). Finally it is a prayer that we may be able to go through the course of our life unharmed by the evil of this world (Gal 1:4).

"For thine is the kingdom, and the power, and the glory forever. Amen."

Although many commentators take for granted that this doxology was appended to verse 13 and did not form a part of the original, it has been accepted and included in the text since the early days of the Church. St John

Chrysostom treats it as belonging to the received text and deals with it in his "Homilies on Matthew". Our Church uses it as an "exclamation" after the recitation of the Lord's Prayer, with the addition of "of the Father, and of the Son, and of the Holy Spirit, now and ever, and unto ages of ages. Amen."

CHAPTER 20

For if ye forgive men their trespasses, your heavenly Father will also forgive you; but if ye forgive not men their trespasses, neither will your Father forgive your trespasses (Mt 6:14-15).

Immediately after teaching His disciples how and for what to pray, the Lord singles out one of the petitions, the one in which we are taught to ask for forgiveness, as if to emphasize its primary importance. (In verse 12, the Lord had called our sins "opheilema" [debts] and here He uses "paratoma" —literally, "a false step, a lapse, a slip".) He had already said that we should ask for forgiveness only if we ourselves are disposed to forgive. Now He goes even farther, leaving no doubt about what is required for receiving forgiveness of our sins and offenses against others. We cannot expect to be forgiven if we ourselves withhold forgiveness. No exceptions are made: there is no question of that other person's being to blame, or of his deserving or not deserving our forgiveness.

It is obvious that the Lord still has His prayer, the Our Father, in mind as He continues His teaching on forgiveness. It is our "heavenly Father" who will forgive us: the disciples, and we as well, are children of the loving Father in heaven. Our calling is to be where the Father is, that is, heaven. It is as if the Lord said, that with such a

Father and with such a calling, it would not be fitting for us to have any other aim for our lives than to be godlike. "And nothing makes us so like God as being ready to forgive the wicked and the wrongdoers; even as indeed He had taught before, when He spoke (Mt 5:45) of His 'making the sun to shine on the evil and on the good'" (St John Chrysostom, Homily 19, *On Matthew*).

"Moreover when ye fast, be not, as the hypocrites, of a sad countenance: for they disfigure their faces, that they may appear unto men to fast. Verily I say unto you, They have their reward" (Mt 5:16). We note here, first of all, that the Lord says, "when ye fast," indicating thereby that He in no way will do away with the ancient pious practice of abstinence. Later He will state even more plainly and emphatically that fasting will be practiced by His disciples (Mt 9:14).

We often assume that the Lord is doing nothing more than warning us of the dangers into which conscientious Christians may easily fall—of making a kind of display of our piety—and that He is speaking only to those who truly fast. Although it is true that such a caution is given here, St John Chrysostom points out that there is implied another thing that is worse: pretending to fast, wearing the "sad countenance of fasting and yet not fasting at all, cloaking themselves with an excuse worse than their sin" (Homily 20, *On Matthew*). In any case, as with any other display of piety, the reward sought, that is, the praise and admiration of others, is indeed the only reward such actors (hypocrites) get.

The Lord has used the plural to emphasize the fact that the whole community of His disciples worships in their deeds and devotions, but now He addresses each one of us in the singular to show that we have our own personal responsibility in all these things. "But thou, when thou fastest, anoint thine head, and wash thy face; that thou appear not unto men to fast, but unto thy Father which is in secret: and thy Father, which seeth in secret, shall reward thee openly" (Mt 6:17-18).

The injunction to "anoint thine head, and wash thy face" is not to be understood literally any more than "entering into thy closet and shutting the door." Christians should neither be ashamed of these good works, fasting and praying, nor should they be afraid for others to find out that they do them. The point is that it is what is in the heart that matters. Christians enter into an intimate relation with God: they pray because of their love for Him; they fast because their whole material, physical life is brought under control and made subject to their spiritual life. Food is the one absolutely necessary thing for maintaining that physical life, and our use of it becomes a sign of its relation to the spiritual life.

The Lord's whole teaching concerning almsgiving, prayer and fasting is summarized in verse 19-21: "Lay not up for yourselves treasures upon earth, where moth and rust doth corrupt, and where thieves break through and steal. But lay up for yourselves treasures in heaven, where neither moth nor rust doth corrupt, and where thieves neither break through nor steal: for where your treasure is, there will your heart be also." It is clear then that in order to possess the Kingdom of God one must be totally transformed. The three acts of piety to be practiced by Christians—true almsgiving, true prayer and true fasting—are at once the means of achieving that transformation and the signs of its taking place. Our destination is that Kingdom: the pilgrim who sets

out on the road to the Kingdom must free himself from
every enslavement, whether to riches, vainglory or reputation. The treasures for himself on earth are fragile and
can be easily taken away. The real treasure is all that
which prepares us for life in God's presence in His Kingdom, whether here in anticipation or in the age to come.
These treasures are spiritual, but secure and enduring;
they cannot be taken away. If wealth (greed), vainglory
(pride) and reputation (disregard for all except for oneself) are someone's real treasure, there is his heart; and
He has not God, but has some idol in God's place.

CHAPTER 21

*The light of the body is the eye: if therefore thine eye
be single, thy whole body shall be full of light. But if
thine eye be evil, thy whole body shall be full of
darkness. If therefore the light that is in thee be
darkness, how great is that darkness* (Mt 6:22-23).

These two verses complete the thought introduced in the
paragraph contained in verses 19-21: "Lay not up for
yourselves treasures upon earth...for where your treasure is,
there will your heart be also." And now, in order to make the
disciples understand better the spiritual treasure that one
should lay up for himself, the Lord moves to a physical image.
The first affirmation, "the light [lamp, from *luchnos*] of the
body is the eye," means that sight generally conditions and
determines the movements and abilities of the whole body.
The point, however, is to illustrate that what the mind (or
heart) is to the soul the eye is to the body. This is evident from
the statement that follows: "If therefore thine eye be single,
thy whole body shall be full of light." The Greek word *haplous*

is, in our opinion, properly translated "single," meaning "singleness of mind, of vision, of purpose and of conviction." It has related meanings such as "integral" or "sincerity." Some translators have gone afield in using "generous," "sound," or "health" as its equivalent—not that these are entirely wrong, but it seems important to us to retain the idea of singleness for the context.

If one's treasures are entirely earthly (see verse 19), his eye is filled with the vision and delight of those things, and the heart (mind) takes delight in them. If his heart is pure or clean, he is blessed, and "he shall see God" (Beatitude 6; Mt 5:8). The reverse is also true: if he sees God only and takes delight in his Law, his vision of his earthly treasures does not compete with his vision of God—hence, the appropriateness of the eye's being "single." The Lord is already anticipating the ultimate truth that He will declare a little farther on: "A man cannot serve two masters...ye cannot serve God and mammon"(verse 24).

The whole body is full of light, the light of God, as a consequence of this singleness of vision. Although the mind is responsible for sin, it is the body that carries out the sinful intention. So the body, whose lamp or light is the eye, is directly involved either in righteousness or in sinfulness.

The opposite of this "singleness" is evil: "if thine eye be evil, thy whole body shall be full of darkness." Then it does not matter how healthy the body may be physically; if godless vision, those earthly treasures laid up on earth, fills the eye, the body responds to that vision giving itself wholly to sin—and what could have been light becomes darkness: "Take heed therefore that the light which is in thee be not darkness" (Lk 11:35).

The person who, trying to be a Christian, is torn between his love for God and his love for the things of this world, ends up with a kind of double vision whereby he finds himself in a terrible state of confusion. He can no longer distinguish between earthly treasure and heavenly treasure. "Woe unto them that call evil good, and good evil; that put darkness for light, and light for darkness; that put bitter for sweet and sweet for bitter" (Is 5:20). This is perhaps the greatest dilemma for the modern Christian: thinking that, in spite of what the Lord says, he can lay up treasures for himself on earth and in heaven at the same time. This kind of division of way of life and of loyalty is no more acceptable in our times than in the time of the Lord's earthly ministry. Times and conditions have changed, but the relation between God and man, and God's demands on man, have not.

The light that has become darkness and has filled the whole body is called a great darkness, because in it there is no light at all. St John sums up the Christian message this way:

> This then is the message which we have heard of Him, and declare unto you, that God is light, and in Him is no darkness at all. If we say we have fellowship with Him, and walk in darkness, we lie, and do not have the truth; but if we walk in the light, as He is in the light, we have fellowship one with another, and the blood of Jesus Christ his Son cleanseth us from all sin (1 Jn 1:5-7).

> No man can serve two masters: for either he will hate the one, and love the other; or else he will hold to the one, and despise the other. Ye cannot serve God and mammon (v.24).

The Lord taught His disciples in the Sermon on the Mount of the nature of the conversion that would make them children of the kingdom of God. He showed them how that conversion would manifest itself in their values, their attitudes, their relations with others, in short, in their whole life. He goes on then to reveal to them the way of perfection—little by little He had led them from one idea to another, always with the purpose of showing them the ultimate demand of God on man.

Inevitably, for the one who sets out to serve God and live in accordance with His commandments, there will be an encounter with the forces of evil that will produce a tension between his love for Him and his attraction to the transitory things of this world.

Everything that He has said before is now brought to its high point with the simple declaration that no man can serve two masters. One of these masters is the tyranny of gold (mammon). This master is capable of destroying finally in its slaves any love for God. Tragically, there are those who think of themselves as exceptions to the rule that one cannot have two masters. St John Chrysostom, in a paraphrase of the Lord's words, summarizes His meaning:

> Thus, wealth hurts you not in this way only, that it arms robbers against you, not in that it darkens your mind in the most intense degree, but also in that it casts you out of God's service, making you captive of lifeless riches, and in both ways doing you harm, on the one hand, by causing you to be slaves of what you ought to command; on the other, by casting you out of God's service, whom, above all things, it is indispensable for you to serve (Homily 21, *On Matthew*).

CHAPTER 22

Therefore I say unto you, Take no thought for your life, what ye shall eat, or what ye shall drink, nor yet for your body, what ye shall put on. Is not the life more than meat, and the body than raiment? (Mt 6:25)

As the introductory "therefore" shows, this command of Christ is directly related to the preceding declaration. "Ye cannot serve God and mammon." He goes on to tell us what serving mammon consists of, lest someone should think that he is not guilty of trying to do just that.

The two words "serve" and "mammon" need some explanation for us to be able to understand the whole passage introduced by verse 25. The Greek verb *douleuein* (which we translate "serve") is related to *doulos* ("servant" or "slave"), and however we may envision our relationship with God, the Lord tells us that God's requirement for us is that we be His servants or slaves. The apostles regularly began their epistles with titles such as "Peter, a servant or slave of Jesus Christ." "Mammon" is the Aramaic (and Hebrew) word for riches, and is used untranslated in the Greek text of the New Testament. It may mean money, possessions or property. All of these meanings come down to one thing: whatever a person owns or possesses, whether it be a great deal or a small thing. No matter how small it may be according to our standards, if we become enslaved to it, it becomes "mammon" for us, our wealth, and finally our god. Thus, being God's slave and the slave of mammon at the same time is impossible.

In the verse quoted above, we hear the Lord telling the disciples and, of course, us, how even the most unexpected things can become "mammon." Again, we should take note of the two principal words in the first line: "take no thought" and "life."

The Greek word *merimnate* means more than "think;" it is "be overanxious" or "be too concerned" about something. It denotes an anxiety or obsession that distracts one from his purpose and divides his interest. (Remember what was said before: "If thine eye be single...") *Psyche* can mean both life and soul; here it is life, the opposite of death, or animate existence. It is the life that God has given man and the life over which He is Master.

This command of Jesus is easy to understand; but it may seem surprising that He has singled out two universal and essential features of our life to illustrate the danger of falling into service to mammon. How does meeting the need to nourish and clothe ourselves become a barrier to our service to God? The answer is simple: excessive anxiety about these two things can turn something perfectly normal and blessed by God into something abnormal and condemned by Him. "For many walk, of whom I have told you often, and now tell you even weeping, that they are the enemies of the cross of Christ: whose end is destruction, whose god is their belly, and whose glory is in their shame, who mind earthly things" (Phil 3:18-19) "I will...that women (and men) adorn themselves in modest apparel,...not with braided hair, or gold, or pearls, or costly array" (1 Tim 2:8-9).

It is undoubtedly true that there has always existed a temptation, even among Christians, to make food and clothing something much more than a simple response to the need to eat and be covered. In modern society, the public is bombarded with advertising designed to create an obsession with elaborate clothing and fancy foods. The average Christian accepts almost without question the standards (our "high standard of living") with which such advertising indoctrinates him. (The advertising industry excuses itself by claiming that it merely reflects the demands of society.) Many Christians see no conflict between their excessive anxiety about food and clothing and their Christian principles. Some point out defensively that only the cults require simplicity and modesty, a radical change of lifestyle in response to their faith. (While it is true that many cults do demand denial or sacrifice of certain things, it is because, for them, those things are evil in themselves. In the Christian faith, it is the use to which things may be put that makes them evil.)

In the early Church, a certain simplicity in all aspects of life was generally accepted by all Christians. It was only after the establishment of the Church as the state religion and the entry of whole populations into the Church that expectations and standards were lowered, and it became fairly common (and acceptable?) for Christians to indulge themselves in luxury and high living. The ideals taught by Christ and the Apostles, however, always remained in the Church's conscience and manifested themselves in two notable ways: monasticism and the Great Fast (Lent). In both, the call to the simple life is of primary importance. In monasticism, men and women bore witness to the fact that it was possible, quite literally, to follow the teachings of Christ, no matter what society approved of. In Lent, all Christians were called back to the simple life, simple food and clothing, elimination of entertainments, and increased concentration on their relationship with God.

In verses 26-31, the Lord stresses the loving care, the providence, of God. If our heavenly Father "feeds the fowls of the air" and "clothes the grass of the field," how much more will He take care of us who are much more in His sight than they! These creatures inevitably fulfill their intended functions. Man, on the other hand, does not always do so; he is different because he has in him the image of God and his God-given mind and freedom of choice. For him to fulfill his function in life, he needs faith in God. His exaggerated concerns for his welfare, his comfort and his security are evidences of his lack of faith. Christians often live without faith, as if there were no God, and are, therefore, not unlike the unbelieving pagans ("the Gentiles") in their materialism. Practically speaking, they make gods of their appetites, their bodies, and their well-being.

IV

The Path to Holiness

CHAPTER 23

But seek ye first the kingdom of God, and His righteousness; and all these things will be added unto you (Mt 6:33).

When the Lord tells us to "seek first the kingdom of God, and His righteousness," we recall that the underlying theme of the whole "Sermon on the Mount" has been "the kingdom." His first recorded utterance was "Repent, for the kingdom of heaven is at hand;" in this, His first extended sermon, He shows how that kingdom is attained and manifested in the life of those who follow Him.

What He is telling us now is that the thing that motivates His followers is the acquisition of the kingdom. All the worries and preoccupations of this world, those cares and hopes that are earthbound, must be overcome by the Christian, no matter how important or normal they may seem to be. The greatest obstacle in the path of the person who sets out to reach the kingdom of God is anxiety over property and over insurance for the future. These two things can become, almost without our realizing it, our primary objects of devotion. They hinder our spiritual development: how can we reconcile the Christian concept of stewardship of this world's goods with the pagan notion of the selfish acquisition of more and more earthly treasures? How can we put all our trust and dependence on God and still be excessively concerned about security for tomorrow? We cannot forget the severe lesson taught us by the Lord's parable of the rich man who was so successful and whose goods increased so much that he had to tear down his barns and build larger ones so as to store up insurance for a carefree future. "Thou fool, this night thy soul shall be required of thee" (Lk 12:16-21).

What is meant by "His righteousness"? Righteousness is a translation of *dikaiosyne,* a word used frequently in the Old and New Testaments, and especially in the letters of St Paul. It fundamentally means the state of one who lives in conformity with God's will. Among the Hebrews, however, it had taken on a kind of formal, juridical sense. Since the Law was the expression of God's will for man, those who fulfilled the Law, often only in an external way, were counted as "righteous." It is no doubt to this understanding of righteousness that the Apostle refers in Romans 10, when he says: "For they" (the people of Israel) "being ignorant of God's righteousness, and going about to establish their own righteousness, have not submitted themselves unto the righteousness of God. For Christ is the end of the Law for righteousness to every one that believeth...for with the heart man believeth unto righteousness" (vv. 3-4, 10).

"Seek ye first..." The word "first" is of vital importance here. The response of the follower of Christ to His coming to us and setting up the kingdom among us must be to concentrate all his concerns on doing His will. The final realization of the kingdom will, of course, be in the age to come, but we enter it now in the present life, and in our own personal life we must strive to live as children of the kingdom. Anxious thought for the things that preoccupy the non-believer is not worthy of a Christian. So, if the kingdom of God and His righteousness are first in our concerns, all these things "will be added" unto us. In other words, to the attainment of the kingdom will be added all the things that we have need of: He does not mean that we will be rewarded with riches. It takes an enormous amount of faith to live the life of a child of the kingdom; it is without any doubt the greatest possible adventure open to man, for it takes putting all our trust in God and His loving care.

The last verse of chapter six contains two thoughts that are both widely misunderstood, and, if understood, rejected by those people who consider themselves to be practical. But we must realize that the instruction to "take therefore no thought for [or "be not anxious about"] the morrow" is addressed to those who understand that the first rule for their life is to seek God's kingdom and righteousness, to those who have no reservations about putting their whole trust in God, and not to those who would go only halfway and try to combine a kind of dependence on God with a little insurance just in case that dependence "does not work!" On the other hand, this is no justification for inactivity; St Paul corrects this misunderstanding of our Lord's words in II Thessalonians 3:8-12.

"The morrow will take thought for the things of itself." There are many ways in which an uncalled-for anxiety about the future, and an unchristian worry about what is to come, may be manifested. Some people spoil their present by worrying about old age, their health, their job, their relations with others, and even their service to God. In a total commitment to God, with faith and joy, the future is always bright.

"Sufficient unto the day is the evil thereof." This could be said in this way: each day has its own evils (not necessarily "wickedness")—afflictions, troubles, misunderstandings, injustices, bad relations with others, needs, etc.—for such is the human fallen condition. Why not set out, with God's help, to solve those problems we are already experiencing, without adding an anxiety about an unknown future? St John Chrysostom paraphrases the Lord's command in this way:

> This I command, for nothing else, but that I may deliver you from superfluous anxieties. For even if today you have taken thought for tomorrow, you will also have to take thought tomorrow. Why then take on what is over and above today's cares? Why force the day to receive more than the distress which is allotted to it, and together with its own troubles add to it also the burden of the following day; and this when there is no chance of your lightening the other by the addition, but give yourselves over to a desire for superfluous troubles? (Homily 22, *On Matthew*)

CHAPTER 24

Judge not, that ye be not judged. For with what judgment ye judge, ye shall be judged: and with what measure ye mete, it shall be measured to you again (Mt 7:1-2).

St Luke records this commandment as one of a series of concise, characteristic instructions of Christ. His choice and arrangement tell us something very important about the spirit of the commandment not to judge. "Be ye therefore merciful, as your Father also is merciful. Judge not, and ye shall not be condemned: Forgive, and ye shall be forgiven: Give, and it shall be given unto you..." (6:36-38) St Paul, in several places in his epistles, echoes the Lord's words and explores their implications: it is often true that the one who judges another is guilty of the same things he condemns (Rom

2:1), and even if he is not, he must leave all judgment ultimately to Christ, because He is the only one capable of true, impartial judgment (Rom 14 and 1 Cor 4:1-5).

The Apostles and the Fathers of the Church rather consistently remind us, in their commentaries on this command of the Savior, that it is some other person, our brother, that we are forbidden to judge and condemn. Wrong, sinful and evil ways of life (lifestyles!), actions, opinions and movements must not only be recognized as such, but, since they are denials and contradictions of God's will for man as revealed by Christ in the Gospel, they are to be condemned.

There is perhaps no better illustration of the principle involved here in the whole Gospel than the case of the "woman taken in adultery" (Jn 8:3-11). The scribes and the Pharisees, those keepers of the "letter of the Law," had apparently gathered a considerable group of people, young and old, to carry out the punishment prescribed in the Law, stoning to death. But they used the occasion to "tempt Jesus," that is, to find out how faithful He was to the Law. Jesus' terrible sentence, "he that is without sin among you, let him first cast a stone at her," was rather their conviction and indictment, and so they all left, the older and the younger of them, and she remained alone with the Lord. He did not condemn her, but He obviously condemned the sin itself, for He told her to go and sin no more.

The new and higher law revealed by Christ is founded on love, and that love is manifested in mercy and forgiveness. The Kingdom that He set up among men is governed by this law, not by formal prescriptions. The self-righteousness that would lead one person to judge and condemn another is what the Lord Himself specifically

judges and condemns here. The person who rather obses-
sively condemns others for their actions and attitudes is
in all likelihood guilty of the same in some way, or guilty
of some other fault, equally condemnable, that he hopes
to cover up by his intolerance. One of the most common
human failings is to compare one's own shortcomings
with those of others and to find them less reprehensible.

Finally, all judgment belongs to God, and His judgment is "according to truth," as St Paul reminds us (Rom
2:2). Our judgment is never really according to truth, not
only in a situation like the one referred to above, but in
all cases. Our judgment is conditioned by our own sins:
no one of us would be able to "cast the first stone."

Unfortunately and ironically, the period of the Great
Fast or Lent, when true repentance of our sins and greater
love for our brothers are called for, provides us with
many occasions for self-righteousness. This is especially
true with regard to the fasting traditions and attendance at
special services. One must never be anxious about what
anyone else does, only with what he does himself. St Paul
sums up the spirit of the Fast and the behavior proper to
the Christian in this way: "Let not him that eateth not...
judge him that eateth...everyone of us shall give account
of himself to God" (Rom 14:3,12).

> And why beholdest thou the mote [a speck of dust
> or a tiny splinter of wood] that is in thy brother's eye,
> but considerest not the beam [a log or tree trunk] that
> is in thine own eye? Or how wilt thou say to thy
> brother, Let me pull out the mote out of thine eye; and
> behold, a beam is in thine own eye? Thou hypocrite,
> first cast out the beam of thine own eye; and then
> shall thou see clearly to cast out the mote out of thy
> brother's eye (Mt 7:3-5).

The profound and vital lesson for the person who would be Christ's disciple contained in these three verses might be stated in these terms: Before you set out to 'help' others with their moral and spiritual life, before you attempt to correct others, even before you attempt to convert others to His way, see to it that you help yourself, correct yourself and convert yourself.

Sometimes we have much greater faults or sins than those of the persons whom we would help. It is appropriate to take note of St Paul's words to those Jews who considered themselves superior to the Gentiles simply because they were of the chosen people and had the Law.

> Behold, thou art called a Jew, and restest in the law, and makest thy boast of God, and knowest His will, and approvest the things that are more excellent, being instructed out of the law; and art confident that thou thyself art a guide of the blind, a light of them which are in darkness, and instructor of the foolish, a teacher of babes, which hast the form of knowledge and of the truth in the law. Thou therefore that teachest another, teachest thou not thyself? (Rom 2:17-21)

CHAPTER 25

Give not that which is holy unto the dogs, neither cast ye your pearls before swine, lest they trample them under their feet, and turn again and rend you (Mt 7:6).

We must keep in mind that the Lord is speaking throughout the Sermon on the Mount to the children of the Kingdom, His own chosen disciples and those who through them would then come to believe in Him. Not only are these children the recipients of the most precious truth about all that really matters, God, man and life, but they are entrusted with it and bear an inexorable responsibility for it. They have the obligation to witness to it, live it, and proclaim it to the world, and at the same time they have the duty to reverence it, defend it and protect it, even to die for it.

"That which is holy" is first of all the wisdom and knowledge with which those who have received this truth are endowed. Therefore, only those who have received God's truth revealed by Jesus Christ know about God, man and life. This knowledge is holy, not having been discovered or deduced by man, and cannot be tampered with, altered, adjusted or accommodated to man's requirements, it cannot be updated, compromised or compared with other truths. In other words, it is an absolute truth and no one can make it less demanding, so as not to offend. It cannot be picked apart and studied like philosophical ideas or movements. It cannot be put on the level of the teachings of any great religious leader or founder of a religion, even if occasionally certain specific parts of another's teaching coincide with Christ's truth.

"Dogs" may seem to be too strong a term with which to characterize the enemies of the truth, but the Lord used this expression for those who deny His teachings and for those who make themselves unworthy of receiving it. Denial of the truth can take many forms. For example, one may question the logic or consistency or even the practicality of the Lord's doctrine. He may feel that the conclusions he has reached about things are more adequate or satisfying. He may think that the Lord's moral teachings were conditioned by the mores and attitudes of His times. He may consider truth to be relative or the result of historical experience. Finally, he may feel that it is not important what one believes or he may have no interest in the truth. Giving this holy truth to the dogs means, among other things, a persistent attempt to convey the truth to those who obstinately reject it, are incurably ungodly and worldly, and would mock it and "trample it under foot." St Paul tells Titus: "A man that is a heretic after the first and second admonition reject" (Tit 3:10).

On the other hand, this commandment of our Lord has a direct application to some present-day situations. A notable one is the inclination of some Christians to minimize mankind's need for the whole truth. This is the sin of certain types of ecumenism in which "differences" are put aside in the interest of a unity which is false and superficial, and in the interest of acceptance, recognition or some material benefit.

But, someone may say, doesn't our Lord command us to preach what we have heard from the housetops? (Mt 10:27) That certainly means that we are obliged to proclaim the truth publicly and that it is sinful to keep Christ's teachings hidden. We have often acknowledged our guilt in this respect, for few people outside the Orthodox Church know what she teaches. We would sin against this commandment if we would, out of excessive liberalism and openness, hold senseless dialogues with representatives of other faiths whose main purpose is to demonstrate the superiority of their systems.

Another contemporary problem with which we are often faced is that of sharing the holy sacraments with those who are not Orthodox. Because of a new liberalism adopted by some other churches, our Church is often ridiculed for not being in intercommunion with others. The Fathers teach us that giving the sacraments to someone who may not accept the fullness of the faith, about whom the stewards of the mysteries are unsure, or who may have a different understanding of the sacraments themselves, is a direct and serious violation of this commandment. We are not calling those people dogs, for they may be innocent or ignorant. The guilt falls on the one who carelessly dispenses that which is holy.

By "casting your pearls before swine, lest they trample them under their feet, and turn again and rend you," we understand fundamentally the same thing as with "giving that which is holy to the dogs." There is, however, an additional sense in which this must be taken. Those who follow a lifestyle that is in violation of Christ's moral teachings cannot be admitted to the sacraments until they repent and change their way of living. Even if one insists that he is Orthodox, works for the Church, attends the services regularly and contributes heavily, he cannot be admitted if he is guilty of certain types of sinful and unacceptable behavior. This would include those who insist on their right to be adulterers, those who live in some illicit union, drunkards, swindlers, those guilty of abortion or some other form of murder, those who hold hatred in their hearts, are unwilling to forgive, or seek revenge, to mention only a few. The Lord warns us of the consequences of a careless sharing of His holy truth and His sacred mysteries with those who are not able to receive them. They profane the truth, because they do not receive it, and they make a mockery of the holy things, because they do not recognize them any more than a pig knows what a pearl is. They "turn again and rend us," by making a display of our laxity, mocking our carelessness and our failure to stand firmly by the truth.

CHAPTER 26

Ask, and it shall be given you; seek, and ye shall find, knock, and it shall be opened unto you; for every one that asketh receiveth; and he that seeketh findeth; and to him that knocketh it shall be opened. Or what man is there of you, whom if his son ask bread, will he give him a stone? Or if he ask a fish, will he give him a serpent? If ye then, being evil, know how to give good gifts unto your children, how much more shall your Father which is in heaven give good things to them that ask him? (Mt 7:7-11)

Many modern commentators, especially among the non-Orthodox, consider this passage to be a "detached saying," with no relation to the foregoing command not to give holy things to dogs. The holy fathers, however (St John Chrysostom, St Ambrose and St Augustine, for example), see it as an integral part of the whole section of the Sermon that deals with Christian behavior and the path to holiness.

If it were unconnected, it could easily be interpreted as a simple promise to grant any request, as indeed it has been understood by many Christians. The experience of having asked for something (often some material benefit) and not having been granted it has led some to doubt the efficacy of prayer, and others to lose their faith.

Again, we must remind ourselves that the Lord is instructing the children of the Kingdom in the ways of holiness and perfection. Just as we understand that the admonition not to give that which is holy to the dogs and not to cast our pearls before swine has to do with our safeguarding the sacred teachings and mysteries of Christ from being profaned, we must also be aware of the fact that the way in which we most often fail to keep this command has nothing to do with other people or their failings: it lies in our own unworthiness to receive God's truth, our indifference toward it, and our carelessness in receiving His holy things (in the Eucharist).

Therefore, in order worthily to receive and then to communicate that which is holy, we must make God's glory, His righteousness, His holiness the object of all our desire and our will. To do this, we are not "to strive alone, but also to invoke the help from above: and it will surely come and be present with us, and will aid us in our struggles, and make all easy. Therefore, He both commanded us to ask, and pledged Himself to the giving" (St John Chrysostom, Homily 23, *On Matthew*). First, then, we must know that what is most important is the thing we ask for; and that can be nothing but the ability to conform ourselves to God's will for us. Having once realized what it is that we should ask for, we must actively seek it. We must convert our conviction or our mental disposition into action. This is what we find if we seek it: a life that is according to the pattern of Christ. With all this preparation, our will and our activity directed toward God and His righteousness (6:33), we shall finally be able to approach the Lord's door and knock.

> Despond not therefore, O man, nor show less zeal for virtue than some do of desire for wealth. For things of that sort you have often sought and have not found, for even though you know that you are not sure to find them, you still put every kind of search into motion. But here, in spite of the fact that you have a promise that you will surely receive, you do not even exert a fraction of the same effort or show a

small part of that earnestness. For this reason, He said, 'Knock', to show that even if He does not open the door to you immediately, you are to continue your efforts (St John Chrysostom, *Ibid*).

All three imperatives, ask, seek and knock, mean continuous effort: keep on asking, seeking and knocking.

The Lord then illustrates His meaning by a simple example which all can appreciate. A man's son, in his simplicity, asks for what he needs, that is, for what he is aware of needing, bread. He needs to eat, so he asks for bread. The father would not mock his son or deceive him by giving him something that looks like a roll or a small loaf of bread, a stone. Nor would he give him a serpent (probably an eel, not considered fish, and therefore forbidden in the Law), if he asked for a fish. In the same way, if we ask for something we think we need, but really do not, the Lord will not give it to us. If He did, we would be deceived, because we would be receiving from God things that might make us even more worldly than we are: wealth, success, physical well-being, and even health, and as a result disrupt our movement toward acquiring His righteousness and ultimately prevent our union with Him. An earthly parent does respond to his child's desire, when it expresses a real need. The heavenly Father knows what we have need of (6:32), and He surely responds: He gives *good things* (not just anything) to those of us who ask Him.

"Therefore all things whatsoever ye would that men should do unto you, do ye even so to them: for this is the law and the prophets" (7:12).

In this way the Lord sums up the Christian standard of behavior. We must have no other example for our

dealings with our fellowman than the way in which our
Lord deals with us. The "therefore" connects this commandment with all that He has said before. If we expect
to receive when we ask, to find what we seek, and to have
the door opened when we knock, we must give and open
the door to them that need and ask for our help. The law
and the prophets had declared this, but even the people of
God had failed to see it. Now He lays the same obligation,
but even more strictly, on those who would be His disciples and enter into His kingdom.

CHAPTER 27

In saying that doing unto others as we would have them do
unto us is "the law and the prophets," our Lord Jesus Christ
emphasizes the fact that He is introducing no new concept.
The Law had laid out in great detail God's demands on man
with regard to his dealing with his neighbor. (See Lev 19:9-
18.) St John Chrysostom goes even further, declaring that "It
is evident that virtue is according to our nature; that we all, of
ourselves, know our duties; and that it is not possible for us
ever to find refuge in ignorance" (Homily 23, *On Matthew*).
To be sure, if the law of doing unto others as we would have
them do unto us belongs to human nature, it is because the
human being has been created in the image of God.

It is important to note too that certain other religions
have a law that, considered superficially, is the same as
this commandment, but in reality is exactly the opposite
of the law given by God to His chosen people and reaf-
firmed by His incarnate Son at the beginning of His
public ministry. They say, in essence: "Do not unto others
as you would not have them do unto you." If one follows

this precept, he could be content to isolate himself from others, do nothing for his neighbor, even be indifferent to his neighbor's condition, and still be righteous. Christ's way is active, not passive.

> Enter ye in at the strait gate; for wide is the gate, and broad is the way, that leadeth to destruction, and many there be which go in thereat; because strait is the gate, and narrow is the way, which leadeth unto life, and few there be that find it (Mt 7:13-14).

The goal or end of the Christian life is the kingdom of God. This is the "Life" to which the narrow way leads. Christ Himself is the "strait gate" that opens the way that leads to life, for He said, "No man cometh unto the Father, except by me" (Jn 14:6). Those who have chosen to follow Christ have already begun to tread this path, and it is here toward the end of the "Sermon" that the Lord begins to tell His disciples that the way they will follow will be filled with hardships and trials and will not be the choice of the majority.

There is perhaps no instruction of our Lord more obviously applicable to the times in which we live than this. It is so tempting to follow the trends and movements of society rather than to stand firm on unpopular principles. Even some Churches have given in and have adopted popular moral attitudes and doctrinal ideas that are in direct opposition to what our Lord Jesus Christ taught, so great is the pressure to be accepted and not to be different. This development in other Churches does indeed concern us, but it is the effect that it has already begun to have on the members of our Church that truly alarms us and makes it urgent for us to remind the faithful that the moral truths taught us by our Lord Jesus Christ are absolute and, therefore, not to be modified to fit the times. It is apparent to any pastor that many of our church members share the attitudes toward doctrine and morality that prevail in society. Sometimes we are told that our whole system is outmoded and that we had better wake up and change or face the inevitable abandonment of our own people.

To stand against dogmatic and moral relativism puts one in an unpopular minority, even to the point of being classed with members of the strangest sects and any others who try to go against the current. One of the first trials to which a follower of Christ is exposed in our time is the fear of being rejected as someone who believes in something out of the past or as a madman. (Society frequently condemns its dissenters as mad.) Great courage is required to run the risk of society's ostracism.

The narrow or "tight" (strait) gate is the confession of Christ, and the narrow way is the path that one has to follow as a consequence of that confession. We cannot declare Christ to be our Lord, God and Savior and at the same time conform ourselves to the standards of behavior set by the many, instead of to His standards. Few indeed are those who have faith enough to resist the enticements to deviate from that narrow way. The other gate is wide and attractive, because it offers success and the praise of men who choose it and follow it. The average or "normal" member of society most often does just that.

The consequences of a godless society have become more and more obvious even to the most skeptical. We are beginning to witness the destruction to which the broad and easy way leads. Sexual promiscuity, free love and moral aberrations have already taken their toll. Disregard for God's will for man regarding marriage and the family has filled our cities with homeless children and runaways, suicides, and despair even among the young who normally are filled with hope and expectation. The "situation ethics" advocated even by some churchmen (according to which in some situations one may lie, cheat, steal and defraud) has all but destroyed trust, honor and personal integrity in public life. The way that leads to life, to the kingdom of God, is filled with hardships and trials; it takes faith in God and in the promises of Christ to follow it. He has said that His yoke is easy and His burden is light, and all of the difficulties can be borne if one never loses sight of the life that He has promised us.

CHAPTER 28

Beware of false prophets, which come to you in sheep's clothing, but inwardly they are ravening wolves. Ye shall know them by their fruits. Do men gather grapes of thorns, or figs of thistles? Even so every good tree bringeth forth good fruit. A good tree cannot bring forth evil fruit, neither can a corrupt tree bring forth good fruit. Every tree that bringeth not forth good fruit is hewn down, and cast into the fire: wherefore by their fruits ye shall know them (Mt 7:15-20).

Throughout the Sermon on the Mount our Lord speaks of the Kingdom of God, both as a present reality, inaugurated in the world by His coming, and as the ultimate fulfillment in the world to come of God's design for mankind. He describes the life to be led by those who become His disciples and thereby citizens of the Kingdom. He indicates the way that leads to life eternal with Him in the Kingdom.

Toward the end of the Sermon, the Lord speaks of the

things that may be obstacles to those who wish to follow Him. In the two verses we studied in the last section, we find Him saying that one really has to make a deliberate choice, first, to confess Him ("the strait gate") and then to follow Him (the "narrow way").

Since there are so many options open to man, particularly in our pluralistic society, Christ and His way are, for a large number of people, just one the many possibilities for satisfying one's "spiritual needs." From a purely worldly point of view, choosing Christ can be very unattractive; no matter how many attempts there may have been to accommodate Christ's teachings to society's demands, the fact remains that His truth, all that He said about God and man, is the absolute truth, not adjustable to different times and places. He did not tell man what he wanted to hear then, nor does He now: He tells him what God requires of him.

Not only will society as a whole, with its popular movements, its new morality and its general apostasy, make it difficult to follow Christ, but there will also be many eloquent, charismatic and popular leaders who will distort the truth and attract large followings. They might appear to be true messengers of God and to help others to be true disciples of Christ, but in reality they will be the false prophets of whom the Lord tells us to beware. They will deceive the sheep, sometimes deliberately, but often because they have already been deceived themselves.

The "false prophet" was no new concept to the disciples, for in their forefathers' time there were many of them. The people of God were warned about them on numerous occasions. (See Dt 13:1-5; Jer 6:14; 23:16-32; Ezek 22:23-28; Zeph 3:3.) Not only will the Lord repeat this warning (Mt 24:5, 10-11), but the apostles will also tell Christians to watch out for false teachers, apostles and prophets (Acts 20:I29; 2 Cor 11:13-15; 1 Jn 4:1; 2 Jn 7).

The most obvious false prophet is the one who teaches a faith that he does not believe himself. No matter how great his learning, no matter how well he may speak, and no matter how many followers he may attract and be praised for his talents, his lack of faith, and his insincerity can only lead others astray.

St Peter says that just as "there were false prophets among the people, even so there shall also be false teachers among you, who privily shall bring in damnable heresies, even denying the Lord... and many shall follow their pernicious ways; by reason of whom the way of truth shall be evil spoken of" (2 Pet 2:1-2). So the heretic is another false prophet, and his doctrine will be the cause of the corruption of many. The first and principal heresy is, of course, "denying the Lord," or, as St John puts it, "for many deceivers are entered into the world, who confess not that Jesus Christ is come in the flesh. This is a deceiver and an antichrist" (2 Jn 7). Included in this heresy are all the false teachings, ancient and modern, about who Christ is and what His mission is. Many modern "Christian" teachers make the Lord over according to their own ideas or according to the tastes of the time. "They speak a vision of their own heart, and not out of the mouth of the Lord," like the false prophets of old (Jer 23:16).

A false prophet is one who deceives the people about what God requires of them. He makes Him a permissive God, who tolerates and even blesses whatever man takes pleasure in doing. He makes the way of Christ an easy pleasure in doing. He makes the way of Christ an easy religion, pushing judgment, heaven and hell into the background, and effectively contradicts the Lord's saying that whosoever will come after Him must deny himself and take up His cross. He promises instant salvation, material wealth and healings. He may be able to give signs and wonders to support his teachings, but signs and wonders are not always from God, and they definitely are not if they distort the Gospel of Christ. The people of God were warned about this:

> If there arise among you prophet, or a dreamer of dreams, and giveth thee a sign or a wonder, and the sign or wonder come to pass, whereof he spake unto thee, saying, Let us go after other gods, which thou hast not known, and let us serve them; thou shalt not hearken unto the words of that prophet, or that dreamer of dreams; for the Lord your God proveth you, to know whether ye love the Lord your God with all your heart and with all your soul. Ye shall walk after the Lord your God, and fear Him, and keep His commandments, and obey His voice, and ye shall serve Him, and cleave unto Him (Dt 13:1-4).

A false prophet creates the feeling that there is no conflict between the way of Christ and the ways of this world. He disregards the Lord's warning that "if the world hate you, ye know that it hated me before it hated you" (Jn 15:18), and the beatitude "blessed are ye when men shall revile you and persecute you and shall say all manner of evil against you falsely for my sake" (Mt 5:11). In short, false prophets are the ones who say, "Peace, peace; when there is no peace," like the false prophets of old (Jer 6:14).

CHAPTER 29

*Not every one that saith unto me, Lord, Lord, shall enter
into the kingdom of heaven; but he that doeth the will of
my Father which is in heaven. Many will say unto me in
that day, Lord, Lord, have we not prophesied in thy
name? and in thy name have cast out devils? and in thy
name done many wondrous works? And then will I
profess unto them, I never knew you; depart from me, ye
that work iniquity* (Mt 7:21-23).

The Lord has spoken with authority from the beginning of
this discourse or sermon. He, like the prophets before
Him, declares the will of God for man and reveals in detail
what the behavior of those who will follow Him must be. Yet,
unlike the prophets of old, He did not begin His instruction
with any claim that "the word of God had come to Him." He
proclaims God's righteousness and speaks of the Kingdom of
God without appeal to any role that He has been given to play.
He speaks and teaches as "one having authority" (v. 29). and
later it will be said of him, "Never man spake like this man"
(Jn 7:46).

He continually refers to man's relation to God; that is,
to His Father which is in heaven, not yet defining His own
function or place in this relationship. Now, however, in
verses 21 and 22, we find a striking change; He is no
longer the one who simply proclaims the will of God, but
He is the very one who is called "Lord," or will be called
"Lord," by those who desire to enter the kingdom of
heaven. He obviously will be their judge: "Many will say
to me in that day...and then I will profess unto them, I
never knew you..." Later, He will remove all doubts both

about the character of the judgment and about His position as Judge. "When the Son of man shall come in His glory, and all the holy angels with Him, then shall He sit upon the throne of His glory; and before Him shall be gathered all nations..." (Mt 25:31-32).

It is especially important to note that the Lord speaks here of the salvation of some who will in some way in their lifetime count themselves as His disciples. They will know that He is Lord, and will call on Him, invoke His name in prayer. So now we hear Jesus saying that simple acknowledgment of Him as Lord and calling on Him is not enough to gain entrance into the kingdom of heaven. What is it then that one must do to be saved? Nothing could be clearer—he must do the will of his Father in heaven. The profession of faith, the claim to be a follower of Christ must be followed up and backed up by the kind of life (again, God's righteousness) of which Jesus speaks throughout the Sermon on the Mount. We see that faith and works go hand in hand and that the old argument—which is necessary for salvation?— is meaningless. It is inconceivable that anyone would be drawn to Christ, receive His doctrine, confess Him to be what He most definitely claimed to be, and then come to the conclusion that it does not matter how he lives his life, and that, in spite of all the Lord says to the contrary, he will not be judged by the things he has done. Such a person will truly replace God's will with his own; he will work out a different righteousness for himself, a sin of which St Paul accuses Israel (Rom 10:13). (There was, apparently, a confusion between "the works of the law," that is, ritual works or performances, by which one is not saved, and the "good works" that are the products of faith in Christ.)

In verse 21 the Lord speaks of all those who would make the claim to be Christians. In verse 22, however, the stress seems to shift to those who have assumed positions of leadership in the Christian community, or have become active in the propagation of faith in Christ. Now it is easy to see why these rather terrible pronouncements immediately follow His warning against false prophets. Some have indeed prophesied in His name, having misread the Scriptures and having attempted to understand them isolated from their context, the Church. Some "charismatic" preachers have made a full time profession of explaining the Revelation of St John, taking almost all their sermon texts from it, and seeing references to current events on every page. Thousands of people have been misled by this type of preaching and have received a completely distorted idea of the Gospel.

Others have a ministry of casting out demons or of faith healing. Some of them shamelessly deceive through hypnosis or the power of suggestion, and pretend to heal willing collaborators. Some attain great fame and fortune for these things done in the name of Christ. It is to such that He will say, "I never knew you; depart from me, ye that work iniquity."

As with most things, it is easy for us to hear only that part of the Lord's teaching, especially His warnings, which seem to apply not to us but to everyone else. What we must understand here, if we would truly be His disciples, is that He will not accept falsehood and pretense from any of us.

CHAPTER 30

*Therefore whosoever heareth these sayings of mine,
and doeth them, I will liken him unto a wise man,
which built his house upon a rock and the rain descended and the floods came, and the winds blew, and
beat upon that house; and it fell not; for it was
founded upon a rock. And every one that heareth
these sayings of mine, and doeth them not, shall be
likened unto a foolish man, which built his house
upon the sand: and the rain descended, and the floods
came, and the winds blew, and beat upon that house;
and it fell; and great was the fall of it* (Mt 7:24-27).

Thus the Lord brings the Sermon on the Mount, His first
recorded lengthy body of teaching, to a close. It is significant that He does so with a parable—the first—for the parable
will be the means by which He will later teach and illustrate
many of the truths that mankind needs to hear and understand.

Only in summing up His doctrine toward the end of
the Sermon did He claim that the teachings were His own,
as well as His Father's; at the same time, he identified
Himself as the one who finally would pass judgment on
man. Here again, He calls these sayings His own, and, as
we have already pointed out, the people who heard Him
understood that He taught "as one having authority, and
not as the scribes," who could only read the law to the
people. So, in a very subtle way, He has now declared
Himself to be the Messiah, the Son of God, the Righteous
Teacher, that Israel was awaiting.

The parable is simple, but it contains the essence of the
response the Lord expects from man as He reveals God's

will to him: "whosoever heareth these sayings of mine, and doeth them." The apostles will repeat this in many ways—for example: "But be ye doers of the word, and not hearers only, deceiving your own selves" (Jas 1:22).

The Lord has taught in a detailed way the kind of life that a man or woman is to lead. He has shown that this way of His is not a matter of keeping a set of specific requirements, but a matter of conversion, a conscious turning away from the evil ways of this world, being moved by God's love for man, deliberately choosing to live in obedience to His will. In the Sermon, the Lord speaks of our relation with God, and with our fellow man; He reveals the truth about human relations, truth that is absolute and unchanging, because it is a truth that comes forth from God and would be the most natural thing for man, created in the image of God, if man's sin were not in the way.

So the Christian life is the one that is built on the foundation of the truth that Christ teaches. But it must also be built: one consciously adopts Christ's way as his own way, and then absorbs the spirit of this way and makes it his own by experience. This he must do, no matter how impractical it may seem, no matter how unpopular it may make him, no matter how much at odds he may finally be with the society around him as a result.

This kind of Christian life will not be shaken by the great crises that occur in one's life. Whatever calamities may befall the Christian, since the foundation is laid and the house is built on that firm foundation which is Christ, nothing can bring it down. The rain, the floods and the winds (the world, the flesh and the devil) cannot undermine the edifice of faith in and obedience to Christ: no turmoil or affliction, no false accusations or plots, no bereavement, death or loss of friends, no sickness or suffering will destroy the house built on so firm a foundation.

The Kingdom of Heaven, both as the abode of the righteous in the world to come, and as a reality already initiated in this present world, is the recurring theme of the whole Sermon. The Kingdom's final realization will occur in the age to come; the kingdom of heaven on earth is a pilgrim community making its way to that fulness. The pilgrim members who follow Christ have had God's truth revealed to them: they have been given the values and standards to live by. Generally, the Lord has stressed the future reward that awaits those who believe on Him and keep His commandments. St John Chrysostom sees also, especially in connection with this last parable, that this happiness (the rewards and consolations for a virtuous life), which will reach its completeness only in the world to come, will already characterize Christ's true followers in this world. In other words, they will come to realize that virtue and godliness will be far more comforting and rewarding even in this present life than wealth, strength, power and fame. Thus, having built on the rock, the firm foundation, a life that is pleasing to God, they become invulnerable to attack, unswerving in their faith, and unyielding to temptation, doubt and discouragement.

On the other hand, the house with the foundation laid in the sand is easily destroyed in time of trouble or turmoil. The idea contained in this statement could be expressed this way: even the person who believes in Christ, acknowledges Him to be the Savior, may have some reservations about committing himself, or be unwilling to be totally obedient to Christ's sayings. He will fall away and lose his faith when the storms of this life are unleashed on him. This person will be an obedient servant of God until there is a conflict between what he wants to do and what Christ tells him he must do.

The wise person is the one who knows that what he has chosen for the basis of his life—that is, the solid rock of Christ and His doctrine—not only makes him a citizen of God's kingdom, both here and in the next world, but also brings about true happiness in this world, because this is God's design for him. In order to make this choice he no doubt has to risk a great deal, insofar as society is concerned. He has to reject much of the fleeting, illusory happiness that a godless life promises. The foolish man, however, chooses to listen to the voice of this world rather than to the Lord Himself. He takes the easy way, following only that part of Christ's teaching that he finds convenient or appealing, thinking he can have everything the world offers, and still reach the kingdom of heaven. "And that house fell, and great was the fall of it."

CHAPTER 31

The Sermon on the Mount is the longest continuous body of the Lord's teachings recorded in the New Testament. Only St Matthew has presented it as a single discourse; St Luke's Gospel contains many of the same teachings, some in a similar "sermon" (6:20-49), and others distributed throughout his narrative (11:9 and 12:22-31, for example). Some Bible students think that Matthew collected into one sermon utterances delivered on various occasions, and others think that the evangelists recalled and recorded only certain parts of a single sermon in their Gospels. It is probably true that the Lord repeated on more

than one occasion many of these same truths and lessons and
consequently there is little point in questioning the authentic-
ity of any of the evangelists' presentations. Whatever the case
may be, we have seen that there is a continuity, a definite
progression, in the ideas contained in the three chapters (5-7)
of Matthew. Their theme is the Kingdom of God, the nearness
of which He proclaimed at the beginning of His public ministry, and the character and behavior of those who would
become its citizens.

The teachings contained in the Sermon on the Mount
are addressed to those who are disposed to accept Christ's
teachings because of a prior acceptance of Him as the Son
of God, the Savior, Redeemer and Messiah. It was the
disciples who went up to the mountain to hear Him. On
the other hand, the "multitudes" must have heard Him,
for at the end, as Matthew says "they were astonished at
His doctrine."

Even from this detail, it is possible to draw a significant lesson. Jesus continues to address to His inner circle,
to us who are Christians and members of His Church, the
same powerful, revolutionary teachings, and a much
larger crowd, the whole of society, is aware of what He
teaches, even if they do not accept Him as the only
authentic Revealer of God's will for man. Those outside
the inner circle might well wonder why His present-day
disciples so readily accept the standards of this world
rather than His.

Another important point: Christ's standards for
human behavior and His formulas for "blessedness" are
in startling contradiction to the accepted ideas of society.
Therefore, in order to receive His teachings as the only
true guide for the way to live, one must acknowledge Him

to be what He claimed to be: the Way, the Truth, and the Life. In other words, the widespread tendency to see Jesus Christ only as an inspired Teacher or Prophet can lead to despair, for He teaches an ideal which, in human terms and within human capacity, is impossible to attain. What is more, that ideal is not always practical or useful, and following it may put one at odds with society. Only His transforming power and the guidance of the Holy Spirit, whom He sends, can make His way desirable and then attainable.

When the Lord promised to send the Holy Spirit, He was in effect warning all of us that His teachings could not be understood except by the inspiration of the Holy Spirit.

> These things have I spoken unto you, being yet present with you. But the Comforter, which is the Holy Spirit, whom the Father will send in my name, He shall teach you all things, and bring all things to your remembrance, whatsoever I have said unto you...I have yet many things to say unto you, but ye cannot bear them now. Howbeit when He, the Spirit of truth, is come, He will guide you into all truth: for He shall not speak of Himself; but whatsoever He shall hear, that shall He speak: and He will show you things to come. He shall glorify me; for He shall receive of mine, and shall shew it unto you. All things that the Father hath are mine: therefore said I, that He shall take of mine, and shall shew it unto you (Jn 14:25-26; 16:12-13).

The Sermon on the Mount is more than the "compendium of the teachings of Christ," more than "the Magna Charta of the Kingdom," more than "the manifesto of the King," all of which it has been called. It is the direct encounter of the human race with revealed truth. The

Word of God had spoken to Moses and had revealed the essence of God's demands on man. Moses and all those men of God who followed Him in the course of Hebrew history spoke with authority, but with an authority that had been given to them and to which they had to appeal. Now that same Word of God, the divine Lawgiver, having taken on human nature and having entered into human history, speaks directly to the human race. He is the authority, and all those who heard Him were aware of the difference between this Teacher and all the other teachers they and their fathers had known. He reveals here, at the beginning of His ministry among men that if man is to fulfill his destiny as the one created in the image of God, his life must be grounded in love of God and love of his neighbor. The precepts and laws of the Sermon are not standards worked out by the human race, but rather the eternal, absolute truth of God.

With respect to women, Jesus showed Himself to be a teacher who overturned popular religious, moral and social attitudes. What was said at the end of the Sermon of the Mount—"the people were astonished at His doctrine" (Mt 7:28)—could describe the reaction of the people to His whole teaching ministry. The officers, whom the chief priests and the Pharisees had charged with arresting Him, in answer to their question, "why have ye not brought Him?" could only answer, "Never man spake like this man" (Jn 7:46).